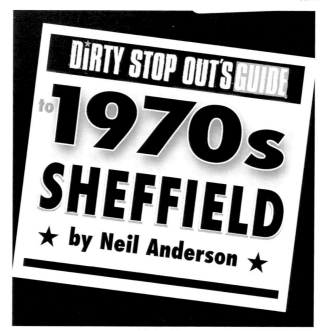

DIRTY STOP OUT'S GUIDE
to 1970s SHEFFIELD
★ by Neil Anderson ★

Published by

★ACM ЯETRO

Dancing the night away, Bavarian-style, courtesy of Hofbrauhaus on Eyre Street

Published by ACM Retro Ltd,
The Grange,
Church Street,
Dronfield,
Sheffield S18 1QB.
ISBN: 978-0-9563649-2-0

Visit ACM Retro at: www.acmretro.com
Published by ACM Retro 2010.
Neil Anderson asserts the moral right to be identified
as the author of this work.
A catalogue record for this book is available from the British Library.

Front cover shot: Go go dancing competition at the Penny Farthing in 1970

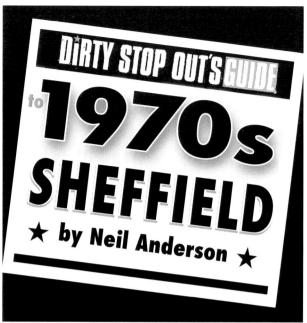

DiRTY STOP OUT'S GUIDE to 1970s SHEFFIELD
★ by Neil Anderson ★

Published by

A busy night at Owlerton Stadium

Joe Cocker gets a cup of tea from his mother which was probably the calmest point in a troubled decade for the Sheffield star that saw him get his marching orders from Australia

CONTENTS

★ Intro — P9

★ Sheffield's date with Elvis

Chapter 1 — P13

★ Club Fiesta: 'biggest night club in Europe'

Chapter 2 — P19

★ Strippers, charity drinking marathons and a world bereft of political correctness

Chapter 3 — P25

★ Crazy Daizy,'Big' Ray Stuart and the launch of Radio Hallam

Chapter 4 — P31

★ Punk snarls at the Black Swan and rebellion gets a home at The Limit

Chapter 5 — P37

★ Sheffield goes all sophisticated - enter Josephine's

Chapter 6 — P43

★ Show me the way to chart success

Chapter 7 — P49

★ Virgin, Bradley's and other purveyors of quality tunes

Chapter 8 — P55

★ Penny Farthing and a rollicking Bavarian style night next door

Chapter 9 — P62

★ Gone to the dogs

Chapter 10 — P68

★ Getting shipwrecked at The Buccaneer

Chapter 11 — P72

★ Penthouse, Wapentake and gigs at Sheffield City Hall

Chapter 12 — P79

★ Spinning the discs at 'Steely's' and 'Improvision'

A busy night at Buccaneer Bar on Leopold Street

Training to pay for a night out in 1976 - a job creation scheme at Meynell Youth Club

SHEFFIELD'S DATE WITH ELVIS

What chance he'll come to Sheffield to sing?

START saving now if you want to see Elvis Presley in Sheffield.

If he comes, expect to pay £30 for a seat at the Club Fiesta.

This is the sort of price that the Fiesta will have to charge to get anywhere near breaking even, if they succeed in bringing Elvis to Sheffield.

Mr. Keith Lipthorpe, chairman and joint managing director, said they would have to pay more than £200,000 for a week's gig by the 37-year-old show business enigma.

"It would have to be an exclusive appearance, so we could attract people from all over Europe and charge between £20 and £30 to make it an economic proposition," said Mr. Lipthorpe.

If Elvis could be persuaded to come, it would be his first-ever performance outside America. In Las Vegas he commands more than £250,000 a week.

club, has seating for about 1,200.

Mr. Lipthorpe is still awaiting a reply. If one isn't received this week, a campaign will be mounted, beginning with telegrams asking for an answer. Also to be considered is a trip by one of the Fiesta directors to see Elvis and Col Parker.

The Fiesta's agents in Los Angeles are in touch with Col Parker. And an invitation has been issued to come and inspect the club.

Money isn't the problem, though. All sorts of offers have been made to Elvis and his manager, Col Tom Parker, in the past. "He probably doesn't like travelling," said Mr. Lipthorpe.

Club Fiesta sent a letter inviting Elvis here two weeks ago, after The Star had pointed out that Col Parker's excuse that there wasn't a suitable supper club with seating for over 1,000 diners in Britain wasn't true. The Fiesta, Europe's largest night

Newspaper article about Elvis at Club Fiesta

There's no doubt Club Fiesta was the city's crowning glory when it came to nightlife in the seventies.

The fact it was proclaimed Europe's largest nightspot when it opened was typical of the confidence in the city at the time.

The venue was that cocksure of itself it even held open a date for Elvis.

The King himself never made it, but the fact the venue had the audacity to raise their head above the parapet and invite him shows the level they were operating at.

Club Fiesta staged performances by virtually every big name cabaret artist of the era – everyone from Tommy Cooper to Roy Orbison graced the stage.

If you fancied a bite to eat before your cabaret performance you could do far worse than sampling one of the many new Chinese restaurants like Zing Vaa and Golden Dragon that were the mainstay of the city's streets or grab steak, chips and peas at your local Berni Inn, which was another seventies hit.

If cabaret didn't do it for you then Sheffield City Hall or the Black Swan probably did: the former for the big live acts and the latter welcoming The Clash for their world debut supporting another bunch of rookie Londoners, the Sex Pistols.

You'd probably be getting your music from Virgin at the bottom of The Moor or maybe Bradley's on Fargate. The likes of Sexy Rexy and Western Jean Company would ensure you were well turned out for the occasion.

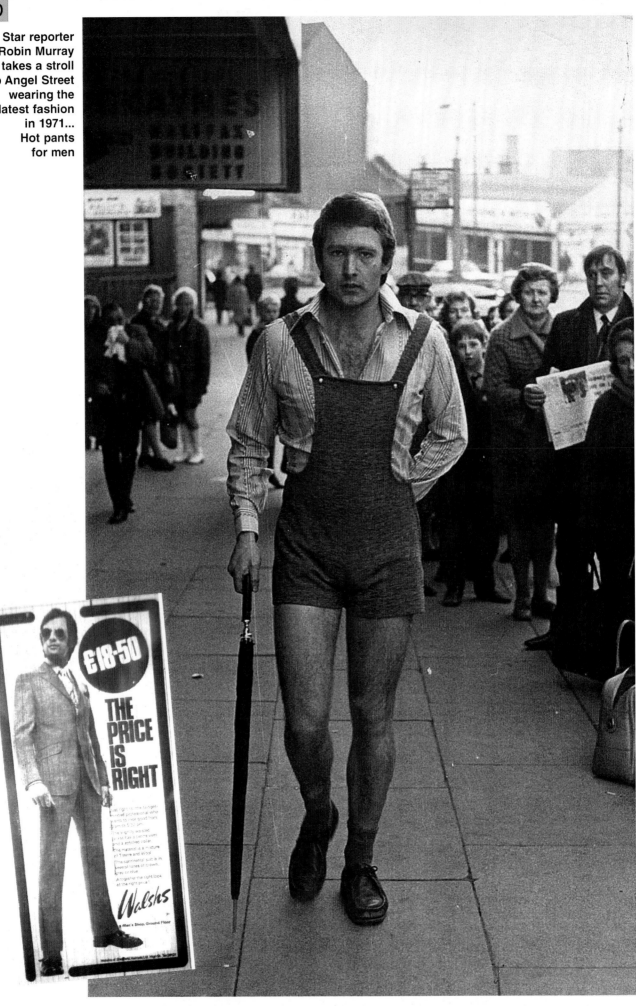

Star reporter Robin Murray takes a stroll up Angel Street wearing the latest fashion in 1971... Hot pants for men

If you felt a dash of sophistication in the air you could do worse than go for a dinner and dance at the Grand Hotel whilst all mayhem was breaking loose at its alter ego - The Buccaneer Bar downstairs.

The kids were far better equipped to hit the town in the seventies – training started early.

★ "There was so much on offer you could more or less go to a different place every night – and we often did!"

Doug Huntingdon

The Top Rank had been promoting matinee performances, with the big hitters from the glam rock scene, for the youngsters since the early 1970s.

If you'd got wheels there was excuse-a-plenty to get out and about for a night out.

Five Ways Motel at Owler Bar (which later became Fannys) was packing them in every weekend.

The Rising Sun on Abbey Lane was the meeting place for millionaire wannabes and the bar under the Beauchief Hotel pulled crowds from the four corners of the city.

One of the biggest events of the era was the 1976 opening of Josephine's in Barkers Pool.

Rotherham's finest lady taxi drivers were always on hand to ensure you got home in one piece, March 1971

**Above:
The iconic 'Hole In The Road' complete with mesmerising fish tank**

**Below:
A typical scene on a Saturday night**

Whilst most of the country was busy sticking safety pins in its lapels, in honour of the punk rock explosion, local business-man Dave Allen went for a champagne bar, restaurant and up-market nightclub and set his stall out for the next 25 years.

If you didn't fancy spending hard earned cash on hours of drinks, food and all-round need-less banter, with the sole aim of persuading the object of your desire to de-robe, the seventies was the place for you.

No need to disappear to Attercliffe under the cover of darkness, it was all here in the city centre. Strip shows were more common place than Starbucks are today.

Soft porn was in full view on the silver screen at the Wicker and drinking competitions got you a pat on the back from your local charity, rather than a flea in the ear from your local health spokesperson.

All in all it was fun enough to forget all the other politically-charged mayhem of the era including Bloody Sunday, the three day week, Margaret Thatcher taking charge of the Conservative Party, the 'Winter of Discontent' and the high pro-file assassinations of Lord Mountbatten and Norris McWhirter.

Ladies and gentleman – welcome to the Dirty Stop Out's Guide to 1970s Sheffield.

CLUB FIESTA: 'BIGGEST NIGHT CLUB IN EUROPE'

I t's unlikely Sheffield will ever have a venue like Club Fiesta again. It was as near as the city will ever get to having a large piece of Las Vegas glitz in the middle of town.

Club Fiesta sat on Arundel Gate and was an indication of the city's confidence in the summer of 1970, when it first opened its doors.

Club Fiesta was Sheffield's absolute piece de resistance of the era in terms of entertainment.

It immediately became a showpiece for the city and the country.

The lavish 1,500 capacity venue boasted an all-seater, amphitheatre-like layout that put the front rows of the audience within yards of the biggest names on the planet.

There was a plush restaurant, in house discotheque and approximately 150 staff on duty each night to ensure the smooth running of the place.

Club Fiesta persuaded the biggest American acts in the world to perform up close and personal with Sheffield: Stevie Wonder, Four Tops, The Beach Boys and The Jacksons, complete with Michael Jackson, were just a few of the household names to make the trip.

Massive home-grown acts included regulars like Tommy Cooper, Les Dawson, Bruce Forsyth and the city's own Tony Christie.

Another Sheffield talent, Marti Caine, started at the venue as a compere and ended up headlining the place.

Top:
Sheffield star Marti Caine who started out as Club Fiesta compere and ended up headlining in her own right

Left:
A busy night at Club Fiesta

Above: Club Fiesta was the brainchild of Jim and Keith Lipthorpe, who'd had their first Fiesta venue in Stockton-on-Tees.

Above: Opening of the Fiesta Club in 1970

Below: Bruce Forsyth backstage at Sheffield City Hall

Christine Ward (who was Christine Milner at the time) started at Club Fiesta when it opened in 1970.

She was the venue's assistant manager and has fond memories of the place.

She said: "The Shadows played the first night at Club Fiesta following its official opening by the Mayor.

"It went well at first and then things drifted a bit. It was land-ing the Four Tops that did it – they could have done a month. They sold the place out and the atmosphere was unbelievable. That's what Club Fiesta needed – top artists.

"When Stevie Wonder came we had to bring in extra doormen to stand around the stage to ensure nobody rushed it. By the end of it even the doormen were stood on the tables dancing! It was the most electric night.

"It was the same with the Beach Boys. I thought they were never going to be able to reproduce what they produced on record, but they did.

"Club Fiesta was the place to come.

"Acts would probably do a week with us and then go home – they wouldn't do a tour as such. They'd also do a regular summer season and some-times pantomime."

But not everyone liked the idea of performing at the cabaret-style of Club Fiesta.

T-Rex, who were at the height of their fame when they were booked to play, definitely didn't.

Christine Ward: "Everything always went wrong when I was on duty on my own.

Members of The Star's Womens Circle filled Club Fiesta nightlcub to watch The Bachelors in January 1971

Club Fiesta
ARUNDEL GATE, SHEFFIELD, TEL. 70101

*

CABARET

WEEK COMMENCING
SUNDAY, 26th NOVEMBER, 1972

JACK JONES
EDDIE FLANAGAN
KIM KENT

WITH THE COMPLIMENTS OF

Club Fiesta

D 16
(6)

ARUNDEL GATE, SHEFFIELD, S1 1DL, TEL. 70101

"For one night only we'd got T-Rex. I arrived about six-o-clock in the evening and at 7.30pm their manager came to me and said 'they're not going on'. It was a sell-out and they were due on at 9pm. They decided it wasn't their type of venue.

"I rang comedian Jack Diamond who I knew was in Sheffield and I said 'Jack you're going to have to do me the biggest favour you'll ever do me – the main act's not going on and I need you to come and do it for me'.
I didn't tell him who it was that was refusing to go on.

"As he came in he saw T-Rex.

"He went to the dressing room and was violently sick and wouldn't go on. I said 'you've got to do it – this is your big chance and we can get a lot of publicity out of it'.

"Jack was introduced and someone shouted 'Ride a White Swan'. And he said 'you ride what you want dear and I'll ride what I want'."

Jack won plaudits for his performance under pretty difficult circumstances.

Legendary British comedian Tommy Cooper was a firm favourite at Club Fiesta and he struck up an unlikely friendship with Christine. It started after she was left to mind him and she took him for a curry on Langsett Road late one Sunday night.

★ "Everything always went wrong when I was on duty on my own. For one night only we'd got T-Rex. I arrived about six-o-clock in the evening and at 7.30pm their manager came to me and said 'they're not going on'. It was a sell-out and they were due on at 9pm. They decided it wasn't their type of venue."

Christine Ward

Fiesta for 1,284 people at the busmen's big night out

Club Fiesta
favourites
Little and
Large

Club Fiesta's own newspaper

★Judi Emm

Author Judi Emm pushed the party barriers more than most in seventies Sheffield. She now lives in Canada but has fond memories of Steel City:

"I worked at the Fiesta and met many stars including The Drifters who became personal friends of mine and often Stretch, the drummer, came to my home and enjoyed himself meeting and socialising with my family.

"God what a blast we used to have, and where did all those wonderful hedonistic days disappear to eh?

"Allan Gee was a disc jockey running a mobile disco called Highway 68 and I was his go-go-dancer, yes I was probably one of the first go-go dancers in Sheffield.

"I was a cocktail waitress at the Fiesta and we were like a big happy family. My manager, who was in charge of all the bars, waitresses and bar staff, could happily drink at the bar downstairs every night while confidently knowing that everyone who worked for him were running the club impeccably!

"I also used to go to the Penny Farthing, Turn Ups, Shades, Baileys, Genevieve, Tiffany's and up-town-Top-Rank-ing.

"I also used to work at the Fargate store Jean Jeanie in the mid-1970s selling Wrangler and Lee jeans. I'd show the girls in the dressing rooms that a shoe-lace put into the top of the zip ensured the jeans always fastened and allowed them to wear one size smaller than normal - that was the fashion in the hedonistic '70s."

NB. Judi Emm's acclaimed 'Olivia's Full Circle' novel has more than a passing reference to nightlife in seventies Sheffield.

Judi Emm
as she is
today

Christine Ward: "The last person the diners expected to walk in their restaurant late on a Sunday evening was Tommy Cooper. He was exactly the same off stage as he was on. I always remember that there was a fish tank in the corner full of goldfish and he said 'well they don't look very lively' and he started poking about in it. Well he had the place in absolute uproar."

She was only ever star struck once at Club Fiesta – by Morecambe and Wise.

She said: "It was my job to meet and greet. They did two shows per night for two nights. I went to their dressing room door and I just stood there thinking 'how can I talk to these icons?'. Somehow they seemed to be above everyone else.

"Eventually I knocked and Eric answered the door and I just couldn't get my words out – I just could not say anything.

"He realised straight away and said 'well hello dear – how are you? What's your name? Come and sit down and have a glass of champagne'. Within five minutes they were my best buddies!"

Club Fiesta even had a starring role in 'City On The Move' (now renamed as 'The

Reel Monty') – the Sheffield Council promo film that ended up fronting The Full Monty decades later.

Sheffield publicity officer of the time, Peter Wigley, admits the venue was his second home.

He even wrote the reference that helped land Christine Ward her job at the venue and famously persuaded Hughie Green to present seventies hit TV show 'Opportunity Knocks'

at Club Fiesta on one occasion.

The massive fees demanded by global megastar acts and the rise of the discotheque were two of the main reasons for the demise of Club Fiesta.

The city still attracts names of global proportions at Sheffield Arena but the days of only a chicken in a basket meal sitting between you and Stevie Wonder are sadly a thing of the past.

**Left:
Peter Wigley –
the man that
helped bring
'Opportunity
Knocks' to
Club Fiesta**

★Dez Bailey

"Our mum took all our family to the Fiesta after my brother Mick's wedding reception. Chicken in a basket was the big thing back then.

"Saw Jimmy Ruffin and the Four Tops there. I never wore a suit after that experience, every time I wore one I wanted to spin round and clap my hands in sync with Mick. Every year there was a rumour Elvis was coming to play there but it never happened of course. He never entered, let alone left the building!"

★Chris Wintle

"Whilst some of the artists were in their formative years the majority simply roll off the tongue – Jackson 5, Tommy Cooper, Bruce Forsyth, Gladys Knight and the Pips, Jim Davidson, Sacha Distel and hypnotist Martin St. James.

"Rumour has it that St. James had people acting out a chicken laying a square egg and shouting 'the Russians are coming'!

"This is nearly as daft as Tommy Cooper who on more than one occasion placed a garden gate in the middle of the stage and just casually kept walking through it and shutting it behind him!

"There was always an excellent house band, led by

drummer Terry Clayton, who always worked with the artist on the night – sometimes with very little rehearsal.

"The only Sheffield venue that came close to Club Fiesta was Baileys but it was always in a far lower league in terms of the acts it attracted."

Inside Baileys

★Nigel Lockwood

"I was 15 and I went to the Fiesta in 1972. I remember one of my games teachers being there and him saying 'what are you doing here Lockwood?' – teachers always called you by your second name in that that era."

Right: The Grumbleweeds and a happily married couple of fans

★Denise Huntingdon

"We'd sometimes go to Baileys. There was a big disco, a smaller one and then live entertainment with acts like Grumbleweeds.

"The Fiesta was strict dress code and top rated acts. We went to see Frankie Valli and stuff like that.

"It was tiered with individual tables and elegant red lamps. It was table service and you could have a meal."

A starry night...

HONEYMOONERS COULDN'T MISS THEIR POP IDOLS DOWN AT THE CLUB

BRIDE Susan Greaves, of South View, Sharrow, and her groom Steven Duroe, of Edale Road, Eccles all (left), were the 'hit of the show at a sheffield club. It was their honeymoon night but they couldn't miss seeing their favourite group, The Grumbleweeds. And the pop lads joined in for a special album picture for their two newly-deeds fans.

STRIPPERS, CHARITY DRINKING MARATHONS

AND A WORLD BEREFT OF POLITICAL CORRECTNESS

W hilst the punks turned veggie and imploded in the 1980s, equal opps ruled the 1990s and the politically correct brigade largely took over 21st century England, things were rather more chilled out in the seventies.

Sheffield nightlife, in some parts at least, was something on a par with The Sweeney on crack – anything went.

Whilst most industries seemed to be on permanent strike and spent most of the decade holding placards outside Sheffield Town Hall, the after dark sector got more and more industrious.

It certainly didn't let incidental issues like blackouts, piles of rotting rubbish, three day working weeks and a 'Winter of Discontent' get in its way.

Dinner time entertainment was a far cry from the

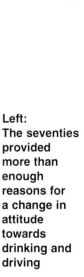

Left: The seventies provided more than enough reasons for a change in attitude towards drinking and driving

NOW OPEN
LUNCHTIMES
12.30 to 3pm. MON to SAT
FREE BEER
TODAY, TUES NOV 2nd, WED NOV 3rd
3 STRIPS
TOPLESS GO-GO
ADMISSION ONLY 5p
PUB PRICE DRINKS
CHEAP PUB GRUB

ROAST CHICKEN	40p
SAUSAGES & MASH	27p
PLOUGHMAN'S LUNCH	30p
STEAK & KIDNEY PIE	20p
SHEPHERD'S PIE	7p

Plus MUSIC, DANCING, TOP D.J
AMERICAN POOL, GAMES MACHINES

HOFBRAUHAUS
EYRE ST. SHEFFIELD Tel. 21807

sandwich and quick wander round town most city centre workers make do with today.

Despite the rise of the feminist movement you could bag three strippers, topless go-go dancer and free beer for only 5p at

Hofbrauhaus on Eyre Street six lunchtimes a week.

Women were praised for undertaking marathon drinking sessions in the name of charity and tales of wife swapping parties in Dronfield were front page news.

DiRTY STOP OUT'S .COM

Protesting on Fargate

Waiting for the bus on High Street

Chris Twiby said: "The whole country was porn and stripping crazy in the seventies and Sheffield was no different. The Wicker seemed to be a mass of soft porn cinemas.

"Strip shows seemed to operate morning, noon and night and beauty contests were common currency.

★ **"Lager was a woman's drink. Men had bitter."**
Doug Huntingdon

"The culture was so different. There was little stigma attached to drinking and driving, smoking was acceptable everywhere and slapping a girl on the backside was taken as a back-handed compliment rather than an immediate disciplinary."

Nightlife entertainment – as still happens in 2010 with the country gripped by recession – was the perfect way to forget the country's problems via flagons of bitter, Pina Colada chasers and a few strippers (both female and male).

The excuses for partying in

seventies Sheffield were actually far more prevalent than they are now.

A whole generation of pubs and Working Men's' Clubs, that were the lifeblood of the era, have gone to the wall in recent years thanks to smoking bans and licensing deregulation.

The 1970s also boasted beer offs, Watney Party 7-packing punters turning up in their droves for student house parties and a very up-market social scene that revolved around the dinner dances of the city centre's Grand Hotel and cocktail parties in the leafy suburbs.

The scene was arguably far more booming than it is today and many miss the easily discernible dividing line between pubs and nightclubs.

Chris Twiby said: "There was none of this deregulation lark, allowing bars to nick traditional nightclub trade by opening all night and everyone having to totally restructure their business to survive.

"You knew where you stood in seventies Sheffield. When the bell rang to call time you were either going to be heralded an after dark hero for downing your drink in one as you headed for a nearby dance floor

or you could end up an after dark zero for failing to finish it in time and be banished to the local chippy."

Vicar will light 'porn' bonfire

By a staff reporter

GIRLIE magazines and pornographic books will be thrown on to a bonfire in Sheffield city centre tomorrow night as part of a Festival of Light nationwide campaign.

The man who will be feeding the fire will be a Sheffield vicar, the Rev. Christopher Whitehead, of St. John's Church, Owlerton.

He will burn half a dozen magazines and books he has bought from shops in the city. But he declined today to say which magazines they were and exactly where he had bought them.

Mr. Whitehead, 36-year-old organiser of "Operation Newsagent," will start the bonfire with wood on a daytime car park at the Devonshire Street - Fitzwilliam Street junction — and will then add the porn to the flames.

Undermining

Newsagents all over Sheffield have been asked to bring pornographic literature to the bonfire. And passers-by will be encouraged to take part.

"This will be a symbolic bonfire to get rid of literature that we feel is undermining the moral welfare of our society," said Mr. Whitehead.

He added that he wanted to protect people from being hurt by pornography and the bonfire would give individuals an opportunity of getting rid of any magazines and books they had bought.

★**"There was little stigma attached to drinking and driving, smoking was acceptable everywhere and slapping a girl on the backside was taken as a back-handed compliment rather than an immediate disciplinary."**
Chris Twiby

DREAMBOAT Norman Mills has got the sort of eyes that make every girl's heart melt. Assistant stage manager at The Crucible theatre, muscular 26-year-old Norman sports a magnificent beard.

Although acting doesn't really appeal to him, he loves the atmosphere of the theatre. A Londoner by birth, Norman worked as a broker for Lloyds Insurance. "But it just got so boring I decided to try something different," he said. "And strangely enough, he landed the job in Sheffield via the Department of Employment.

As for status, well you'll be glad to hear, girls, that Norman is definitely unattached. Those powerful looking shoulders betray his love of sports, particularly rugby.
Amanda Brown

Right: Sheffield's last back-loader passenger bus crewed by Mick Webber and conductress Kath Shea, which retired from nightlife duties in December 1976

Below: Yard of ale drinking – one of the most popular pastimes of the 1970s

The social stigma attached to drinking and driving hardly existed in the 1970s – hence venues like Five Ways Motel (which later became Fannys and is now a rather more sedate hangout in the shape of a cut price carvery) could operate as a popular nightspot with punters driving from miles around.

Mark Shaw said: "Nobody batted an eyelid when anyone

★ **"Fannys? It was full of lairy posh people."**
Joanne Stephenson

drank alcohol and drove in the seventies. It seems absolute madness now. It's doubtful somewhere like Fannys could exist in 2010. The taxi fares alone would be absolutely astronomical!"

Sheffield certainly wasn't an area to let the grass grow under its feet as far as sexual liberation was concerned.

Instead of waiting decades for La Chambre swingers club to open in Attercliffe, it got down to business in Dronfield.

The allegations of wife swapping parties were confirmed by none other than Rev Richard Sledge, Vicar of Dronfield.

He told The Star at the time:

"Yes it exists...It concerns individuals and their families."

The church even ended up offering counselling for its troubled congregation.

The vicar believed the problems stemmed from all-night parties going too far.

He added: "Lots of people have parties at all times of the year. Most parties are just ordinary but why in some places parties go too far I just don't know."

The vicar went on to say he'd been approached by "remorseful men and women" who'd been involved.

The church were also out in force for the arrival of horror smash 'The Exorcist' which was released in 1973.

Martin Bellamy: "The ABC Cinema in town had a big tunnel for people to queue in and when 'The Exorcist' debuted there were nothing but vicars wandering around shouting 'God loves you, don't see this film'."

★ "Nobody batted an eyelid when anyone drank alcohol and drove in the seventies. It seems absolute madness now."

Mark Shaw

★MOTHER MARY'S CHARITY DRINK SUCCESS

Into the bitter battle...

THE LADIES NOTCH UP A RESOUNDING VICTORY FOR WOMEN'S (HIC) LIB

●MRS. Mary Grayson on the winning trail in her effort to sink a yard of ale in the drinking contest.

MEN DO THEIR BEST, BUT IT JUST IS NOT GOOD ENOUGH

OUT TO PROVE THAT THEY'RE ONLY THERE FOR THE BEER

There was a party of different sort kicking off down the road in Gleadless – a beer battle between the sexes.

Mother-of-four, Mrs Mary Grayson, had decided to play the men at their own game.

She out-drank the lot of them to win the yard of ale competition in record time.

The media billed it as victory for women's lib, in a tongue-in-cheek sort of way.

In 2010 the world record for drinking a yard of ale (approximately two-and-half-pints) stands at five seconds. It's unlikely that record will ever be broken – well not if the local health authority have anything to do with it anyway.

Mary didn't beat the world record that night but we understand she didn't spill a drop and she raised a few quid for charity.

Well done mother Mary!

The restaurant at Turn Ups night spot in Nether Edge. February 1977

TurnUps

EVERY
MONDAY TO THURSDAY
Free Admission before 10p.m.

top of the town discotheque

19/21 Nether Edge Road, Sheffield.   Phone: Sheffield 56636.

Dancing at Turn Ups in 1977

CRAZY DAIZY, 'BIG' RAY STUART
AND THE LAUNCH OF RADIO HALLAM

CHAPTER THREE

The 1973 closure of Leopold Street's Buccaneer Bar caused widespread dismay amongst its dedicated and passionate regulars.

In fact the venue's management were that worried about an invasion of souvenir hunters they made the decision to shut the place without warning.

"But despite this the police are still looking for four missing tables", it was reported in The Star at the time.

Trust House Forte, who owned the site, sold it for redevelopment.

Buccaneer Bar did outlast The Grand Hotel situated upstairs but not for long.

The saviour for the lost generation came in the shape of the Crazy Daizy which opened on High Street.

It included the larger than life 'Big' Ray Stuart on the decks with assistance from former Buccaneer Bar DJ George Webster, who went on to open The Limit on West Street in 1978.

Ray, who had success with his 'Frankenstein and the Monsters' act a decade earlier and also landed a job with Radio Hallam, which aired its first programme from its Hartshead Studios on October 1, 1974, was a big pull.

The Crazy Daizy became nationally and internationally renowned as the venue that Human League front man Phil Oakey first clapped eyes on Joanne Catherall and Susan Sulley – the two then school-girls he recruited for his new look synth act that went on to global domination.

It also held a hugely popular midweek 'Roxy Night' named after Roxy Music.

★ The Crazy Daizy became nationally and internationally renowned as the venue that Human League front man Phil Oakey first clapped eyes on Joanne Catherall and Susan Sulley – the two then school-girls he recruited for his new look synth act that went on to global domination.

★

Left: Alvin Stardust and 'Big' Ray Stuart' at Radio Hallam

Above: Mel Day - compere/singer/DJ at Baileys, who helped develop the venue's popular Tuesday 'Crazy Night' complete with horror acts and scantily clad dancers

Sex Pistols at Radio Hallam in 1976

Cliff Richard
and Keith
Skues at
Radio Hallam

Local rockers Panza Division were on the bill alongside Def Leppard at Sheffield Show in Hillsborough Park in 1978
– Radio Hallam were none too pleased at the band sticking their banner over the station's branding by all accounts

UNWIND STEIN & DINE
SHEFFIELD
BIER KELLER
The new night-out for fun lovers

HOT GERMAN
STYLE MEALS
AND SALADS
AVAILABLE AT
LUNCHTIME.

BIER KELLER
11-17 HIGH STREET SHEFFIELD

★NIGHTS AT THE CRAZY DAIZY

Martin Smith first went in 1976.

"Post-Roxy Music, pre-punk and bang in the middle of night club narcolepsy.

"The charts had 'Misty', 'The Hustle' and 'Whispering Grass', we wanted Iggy, Bowie or something, anything, that didn't wear denim flares or a tartan scarf.

"There wasn't much to choose from. For a bunch of boozy chancers looking for more than the Detroit Spinners and less than heavy rock, Crazy Daizy was a suit-free paradise.

"It was cool but didn't try too hard, exclusive but for everyone, arty but full of working class kids with an eye for style and

an ear for greatness.

"Or at least I think it was.

"The truth is memories are few and thin. By the time we walked downstairs into Daizy's throbbing gloom much damage had been done.

"We had Mansfield Bitter after football, Colt 45 on the way up and whatever they had in the Blue Bell and The Stonehouse.

"I don't remember the details of the first time I ever went and I don't remember how many times we went but I liked it enough to drag a busload of mates from Eastwood, Nottinghamshire, up there for my 21st in February 1976.

"I have vague recollections of dancing holding a bottle of champagne.

"The girls were glam in a non-Josephine's way.

The lads looked good without the dreaded night-club suits.

"It was easy really, we just needed somewhere to go.

"Most areas had one pub with a brilliant juke box; some city centre bars had a certain something but nowhere really got it.

★Dez Bailey

"We just loved the Crazy Daizy. A normal Friday night out would be a pint in the Midland at Killamarsh, bus into town, and head for the Old Blue Bell.

"Here a lot of customers looked like Bowie, Rod Stewart, or Bryan Ferry. Big dance floor favourites were 'Suffragette City' by Bowie and 'Virginia Plain' by Roxy Music.

"BBC Radio Sheffield DJ Michael Cook used to promise Rod Stewart but never play it, so we hassled him every week and ended up with 'Maggie May' and 'You Wear It Well'. Saturday afternoons felt as though you were in the evening club; same cool vibe.

"From there you could still get a beer at the Golden Dragon Chinese restaurant off The Moor. This you could spin out till 6.30pm then only one hour before the night session began!"

★NIGHTS AT THE CRAZY DAIZY

"We had worn out Nottingham and tried Coventry, Leeds, Derby, Doncaster, Manchester, Birmingham and all towns between looking for that something.

"We had been to Sheffield before to the queue-up-in-your suit night clubs like Baileys, had the arguments with the bouncers because our lapels weren't regulation or we smiled once too often in the queue.

"We didn't know in 1975 what was to follow a couple of years later; we were followers, not leaders but boy were we ready for a change. The Real Thing and Abba might sound good in retrospect but at the time they were a living death.

"We'd had our fill of the Northern Soul that had been worn out by a million dance steps on every 'disco' floor for five years, great though that had been in its time.

"So, for us, Crazy Daizy was all we were looking for. I just wish we had pictures, but lads didn't generally carry cameras back then.

"Despite the hazy memories there is one abiding image of a kid with a curtain of black hair parted on one side and falling almost down to his shoulder on the other.

"I don't know if it was Phil Oakey because this particular barnet had a single white stripe running through it.

"But I do know that we had a great time every time we went and it goes down as one of the best clubs I ever went to, I think."

★Chris Wintle

"There used to be a big scene in there on a Saturday afternoon. It was quite big but was still a glorified pub. Good pint of lager though."

Above: Crazy Daizy manager David Mearns Jamieson

Below: Roger Moffat and a womble at Radio Hallam

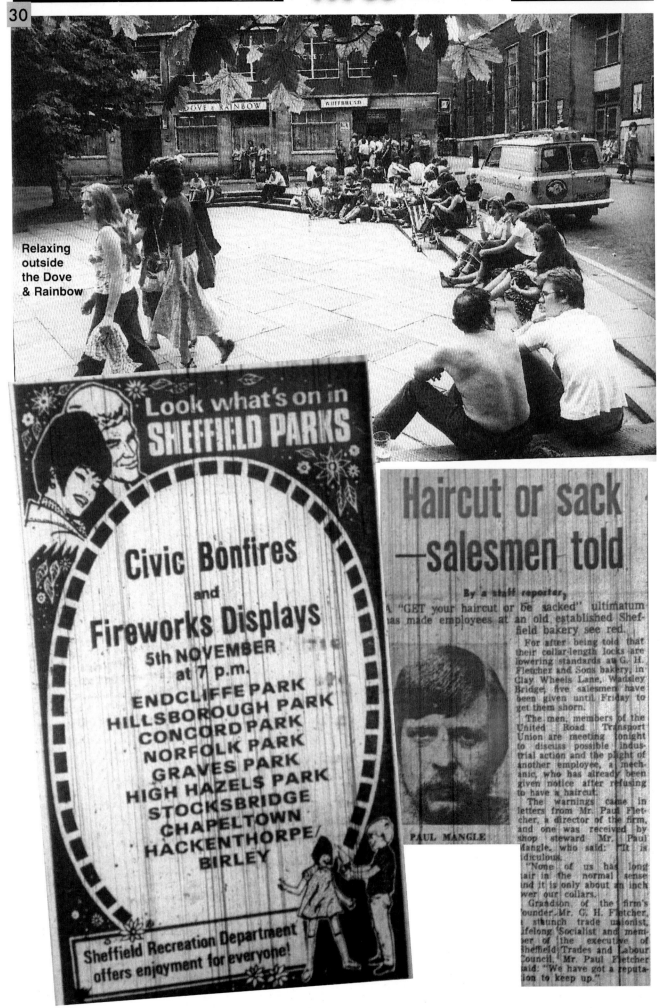

Relaxing outside the Dove & Rainbow

Look what's on in SHEFFIELD PARKS

Civic Bonfires
and
Fireworks Displays
5th NOVEMBER
at 7 p.m.
ENDCLIFFE PARK
HILLSBOROUGH PARK
CONCORD PARK
NORFOLK PARK
GRAVES PARK
HIGH HAZELS PARK
STOCKSBRIDGE
CHAPELTOWN
HACKENTHORPE/
BIRLEY

Sheffield Recreation Department offers enjoyment for everyone!

Haircut or sack —salesmen told

By a staff reporter,

A "GET your haircut or be sacked" ultimatum has made employees at an old established Sheffield bakery see red.

For after being told that their collar-length locks are lowering standards at G. H. Fletcher and Sons bakery in Clay Wheels Lane, Wadsley Bridge, five salesmen have been given until Friday to get them shorn.

The men, members of the United Road Transport Union are meeting tonight to discuss possible industrial action and the plight of another employee, a mechanic, who has already been given notice after refusing to have a haircut.

The warnings came in letters from Mr. Paul Fletcher, a director of the firm, and one was received by shop steward Mr. Paul Mangle, who said: "It is ridiculous.

"None of us has long hair in the normal sense and it is only about an inch over our collars.

Grandson of the firm's founder, Mr. G. H. Fletcher, a staunch trade unionist, lifelong Socialist and member of the executive of Sheffield Trades and Labour Council, Mr. Paul Fletcher said: "We have got a reputation to keep up."

PAUL MANGLE

PUNK SNARLS AT THE BLACK SWAN

AND REBELLION GETS A HOME AT THE LIMIT

CHAPTER FOUR ★

Left:
Siouxsie
plays The
Limit in
1978

Sheffield's own
Bitter Suite that
opened The Limit

**Below:
Nigel Lockwood,
Ann Hornford,
David Webster
and Lesley at
The Limit after a
gig by The
Members in 1979**

Sheffield's contribution to the first wave of punk – on the face of it – was nothing to write home about.

In fact two words – 'knob' and 'all' – listed in that order, are as succinct a conclusion as you need on an embarrassing period in our music making history when we could only look on in envy as Manchester – just over the Snake Pass - was flying the flag for the north with the likes of Buzzcocks and Slaughter and the Dogs headlining punk venues across the land.

Sheffield's staging of The Clash's live debut at Snig Hill's Black Swan, supporting the Sex Pistols, is regularly cited as the city's main contribution to the early punk scene but Steel City actually had a far greater influence in a story that's often overlooked.

Punk would not have had anywhere near the influence it did without a certain Sheffielder who, at the time, looked liked being destined to live out his days on the cabaret circuit.

If it wasn't for the attitude, songs and stage show of a former coke oven worker, Dave Holgate Grundy, punk rock history could have been very different.

Changing his name to Dave Berry (after his hero Chuck Berry), he had his first hit in October 1963 with 'Memphis Tennessee'.

Dressed all in black, he'd regularly hide behind the upturned collar of his leather jacket and was a big fan of wrapping himself around his microphone lead and any other available prop – a stage act totally at odds with bands like The Beatles, The Shadows and the Dave Clark Five, with whom he was sharing the charts.

★ **Punk would not have had anywhere near the influence it did without a certain Sheffielder who, at the time, looked liked being destined to live out his days on the cabaret circuit.**

"A lot of it was anti what you were supposed to be doing at the time", he admits. It worked.

He had a string of top twenty hits between 1963 and 1966 – his most well known being 'The Crying Game' that reached the No 5 spot in July 1964.

But bizarrely, over 10 years later, it was the 'b' side, 'Don't Gimme No Lip Child' that came to real world-wide prominence when it was covered by the Sex Pistols and appeared on 'The Great Rock'n'Roll Swindle' album.

His unconventional stage presence was years ahead of its time and the Pistols quickly acknowledged him as an inspiration.

And word soon spread.

The whole thing became a bit of a shock to Dave Berry.

He said: "One evening at a rock venue in London I was astonished to notice some very odd looking characters at the front of the stage. The punk era had arrived and although I was delighted to see some of them enjoying my show, I couldn't quite work out what the attraction was for them. My road manager

ushered them to my dressing room, saying they wanted to meet me.

"My question to them was straight to the point: 'What are you doing here?'"

They said they were Pistols' fans and wanted to check out the man whose songs they were covering.

Adam Ant was that much in awe he invited Dave Berry to support him at key shows, including London's Lyceum.

"The reviews I received were very special indeed and my daughter Tania couldn't believe it when I took her along to meet Adam", he said.

You had to give him credit – even the gobbing didn't bother him, he revelled in it.

Dave Berry said: "I received my punk badge of honour when the audience spat at me on stage!"

Siouxsie and the Banshees were also fans and The Monochrome Set were regularly performing another Berry hit – 'Little Things'; the tabloid press regularly referred to him as the 'godfather of punk'.

Above: Limit owners Kevan Johnson (left) and George Webster at its 1978 opening

Left: Generation X at The Limit

★BLACK SWAN

Right: Sheffield punks in 1977

Many have argued that it's about time somebody did a book on the legacy of Snig Hill's Black Swan (rechristened the Boardwalk in later years). They're probably right. Unfortunately we're only trying to do justice to a brief period of its years of dominance and influence here.

The renowned venue was run by larger than life figure, Terry Steeples, who was originally working for a cinema chain until "that went down the drain".

Despite the fact he'd never run a pub before things went rather well.

In fact he developed the venue into one of the most successful of its kind in the era.

It was a massive hit with live music fans thanks to Terry's uncanny ability to book the right bands. But it wasn't just bands.

A raucous mid-week hen night, orchestrated by the man himself from the stage, became one of their most popular and most successful events in the venue.

Terry was then asked to run the Merry England Bar downstairs. He enjoyed similar success though he never agreed with the brew-

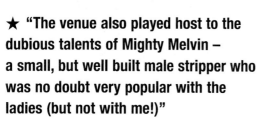

ery's decision on the name.

"It was a bit poofy", he said.

Chris Wintle: "The Black Swan was very central to a music lover's life in Sheffield in the 1970s. During the week the venue would host a lot of local bands mainly playing covers. It was a particular favourite of Sheffield's very own Bitter Suite.

"The venue also played host to the dubious talents of Mighty Melvin – a small, but well built male stripper who was no doubt very popular with the ladies (but not with me!)

"But it was Sunday nights that the Black Swan was my regular place of worship and it was one of the main stop off points for touring pub rock bands.

"One of the main acts that seemed to play there once a month – even though it was actually

once every five or six months – was a band called Brinsley Schwarz.

"Black Swan main man Terry Steeples did more for music than anyone of the era. He was a totally larger than life character.

"He'd book Brinsley Schwarz every week it seemed – they were virtually the house band. They contained Nick Lowe who was the best songwriter in the world as far as I was concerned. They'd fill the place.

"One night Terry said we had to come and see this band from London that he said were set to be the next big thing. I was expecting really good music. I arrived at 7.30pm and they'd brought loads of supporters from London with safety pins stuck all over them. There could only have been 30 or 40 people from Sheffield there.

"Sex Pistols front man Johnny Rotten just stood at the side of the stage and picked fights with people for the entire gig. It was all a bit of a shock to the system.

"Support band The Clash, who were making their live debut that night, were awful. I remember bass player Paul Simonon having to stop to get a roadie to tune his guitar. To us it was just a noise. We thought 'this will never take off'.

"Little did we know they were going to change the face of music.

"When The Black Swan wasn't promoting bands they put on strippers and all kinds."

★ **"The venue also played host to the dubious talents of Mighty Melvin – a small, but well built male stripper who was no doubt very popular with the ladies (but not with me!)"**

Chris Wintle

★Reg Cliff

"I have two vivid memories of gigs at the Black Swan. Being into lots of different types of music, but mainly rock, I was always keen to see what an act was like if it was getting publicity. So that's why I was there on 4/7/76 when the Sex Pistols came to town supported by The Clash. It was The Clash's first ever gig. They were awful. The Pistols took the stage with their followers from London comprising nearly half the audience. I hated them. I put my thoughts into a letter which I sent to Melody Maker and Sounds. They both printed it.

"A month later I went to see AC/DC

for the first time, although not the last. Bon Scott was the lead singer and he had the audience mesmerised. When they came on it was still light and you could see through the windows out onto Snig Hill. A bus pulled up outside, I think it was a number 88! AC/DC finished a song and as the applause died down, Bon Scott spotted the people on the top deck of the bus peering in and he screamed out, 'hello everyone on the bus'. Hilarious to see the astonished faces of the bus passengers as they wondered what this bare-chested rock singer with long hair was doing."

★Ian Gomm of Brinsley Schwarz

"The band (referred to as the Brinsleys) lived together in a commune in a big house in London and whilst we had little money, we decided to go on the road.

"One evening a bloke from Sheffield called the band and said would the band like to come and play a gig at the Black Swan and he sold us the gig on the premise that Joe Cocker was from Sheffield and that he was a pretty good singer!

"My main memories of coming to play at the Black Swan was of the ridiculously long time it took in those days to travel from London and there always used to be a shout of delight when they neared the towers at Tinsley and knew they were nearly there!

"The bloke that sold us the first gig in Sheffield was of course Terry Steeples and he always treated us brilliantly and knew that we would always 'fill in' if a band had cancelled a pre-arranged gig.

"One particular night we asked Frankie Miller to come up to Sheffield with us and whilst Frankie had never played at the Black Swan before he couldn't wait to go there because he had heard of the reputation and the heritage of music in Sheffield, particularly Joe Cocker.

"We would travel up to Sheffield in a transit van, play the gig and then travel straight back down to London – we must have been mad but it was worth it for the great times we had at the Black Swan – I am only sorry that there were no pictures or videos of the Black Swan gigs."

Below:
Mick Shedd
and his Side
Effects at
The Limit

★THE LIMIT

This iconic venue was the brainchild of former Buccaneer Bar/Crazy Daizy/Wapentake DJ George Webster and ex-copper Kevan Johnson.

Wapentake matriarch Olga Marshall was not a happy bunny when bin liner-wearing punks started appearing in her very rock-based establishment.

George and Kevan didn't help matters by nicking most of her staff and employing them at their new Limit venture that opened in 1978.

They did, in fairness, strike a deal with Olga which ran most of the parties involved ragged but kept both venues operating nicely.

Wapentake DJ Paul Unwin, for example, would play his first few hours at Wapentake Bar and then decamp to West Street to play another set at The Limit until the early hours.

Though The Limit was Sheffield first 'official' punk venue and welcomed jeans, pogoing, gobbing and anything else associated with the scene, it definitely played it safe on opening night, March 22, 1978.

Local rock band Bitter Suite played to a packed house.

Paul Unwin, who had also taken on the club's management as well as DJing duties, said it might have looked okay front of house but things didn't go quite so well everywhere else.

He said: "Opening night was a total disaster but the customers wouldn't have known that. We'd come as DJs but we were now asked to be nightclub managers.

"We were trying to get the beer to switch on and the lights to switch off."

Bitter Suite also had their own feelings of trepidation.

Bassist Gerry Scanlon said: "I can remember arriving at the gig for the sound check in the afternoon to find joiners and electricians etc still working and the place was opening in a matter of hours!"

Despite all that it was a great gig.

Siouxsie and the Banshees were the first 'big' punk band to appear following a show by Sheffield act The Push led by future soap star Ray Ashcroft.

Paul Unwin said: "Nobody had seen anything like Siouxsie and the Banshees in Sheffield; she'd just got a single in the charts that was 'Hong Kong Garden' and she was at the height of the punk scene then."

The Limit hosted some pretty impressive – and sometimes bizarre - gigs in the late seventies.

They staged the UK debut of the B-52s, Def Leppard supported the Human League, U2 played to 14 people and the venue became pivotal to the city's electro music dominance of the early 1980s with early gigs by Comsat Angels, Clock DVA and Vice Versa (later to become ABC).

Other notable gigs by Sheffield acts of the era included shows by Artery (with future Limit manager Garry Wilson on drums), The Extras, The Negatives (a band championed by Limit co-owner George Webster) and the Stunt Kites.

Undertones
at The Limit

They nearly hosted a very early gig by heavy metal Saxon (then going under the guise of Son of a Bitch).

Pete Gill, the Sheffield drummer that was a former sticks man for Gary Glitter in the glam rocker's seventies heyday, was playing for them. He said: "We got paid up for being too loud. We went on and after the third number that was it – we more or less emptied the place. I think we took about an 8k rig in there. Kevan Johnson came up and said 'no, no, no – we're not having this. I've got customers to think of. Now get off!'"

But besides that, Pete Gill was still a regular in the place.

He said: "I thought The Limit was one of the best places I've ever been to – both band-wise and vibe-wise. I saw some amazing acts down there."

★COPPERS AND NUTTERS AT THE TOP RANK

Tony Beesley, author of the 'Our Generation' trilogy, said: "I can still see Paul Weller's face now looking up at the two crazy crombie attired skinheads who came bursting into the Top Rank with broken bottles screaming and shouting threats to all and sundry.

"Weller didn't even flinch. The cops followed the nutters in and dragged 'em off, still bellowing obscenities. Outside, my mate John Harrison and his mates were being chased all over Sheffield by skinheads.

"One night in Pond Street my mate Clarkey got a whack in the nose out of nowhere from a kid who was part of a big gang. He was always getting whacked come to think of it, but it never phased him and he kept coming back to watch more punk rock.

"We got chased a few times right to our bus stop. We got threatened a fair few times and dodged scuffles, brawls and near riot sized battles.

"We even saw The Clash's Joe Strummer belt Mick Jones for not wanting to play 'White Riot' for us but we survived... and the music was almost always worth it.

"The highlights of those Top Rank nights were The Jam coming on with 'Strange Town' and the whole place erupting into a pogoing mass; the Damned literally recreating their anthem 'Smash It Up'; the perfect pogo pop of the Undertones; 999 proclaiming 'I'm Alive' and giving us a 'Direct Action Briefing' and The Clash right at the end of the decade.

"If I close my eyes and listen to 'Complete Control', I can still see and feel that experience and the Top Rank comes alive once more; the pulse starts racing, the excitement starts increasing and the mind shifts back to a different time."

★ Nigel Lockwood

"I never saw much trouble at any of the clubs. But when punk went overground with the second wave of the movement in late 1977 I saw a lot more – especially at the Crazy Daizy before The Limit opened.

"Wire were originally down to play the second night The Limit opened but they cancelled and The Push did it. I asked Limit DJ Paul Unwin what his all time favourite Limit gig was – he said Roger Chapman.

"At school you had two camps – one was your Led Zeppelin, Deep Purple, Uriah Heep and Black Sabbath camp and your other was Bowie, Lou Reed and that was me."

Lord Mayor's Parade – a massive event in the seventies

SHEFFIELD GOES ALL SOPHISTICATED
- ENTER JOSEPHINE'S

CHAPTER FIVE ★

Left:
Dancing at
Josephine's
in 1977

Dave Allen (centre) and Josephine's staff

Left: Josephine's staff

When you weighed up the tens of thousands of pounds commanded by the global acts playing Club Fiesta against the cost of a DJ who could pack a discotheque, it didn't take a mathematical genius to work out where the future was.

Sheffield-based entrepreneur Dave Allen mapped things out for the next quarter of a century when he opened Josephine's in 1976. He also brought in much of the glitz of cabaret clubs and then some.

Whilst most nightclubs played at food, he offered haute cuisine and top class service. He installed air conditioning, brought in ice machines and the champagne corks popped from day one.

Dave Allen, who'd already opened Napoleons Casino on Ecclesall Road the year before, said: "I wanted to open a place that people would dress up to come in. The Penny Farthing was the club of the day but you didn't get ice in your drinks. There was no air conditioning and it was all hot and sweaty.

★ **"I think it was well known that if you were going to Josephine's you had to get dressed up as if you were going to a wedding."**

Dave Allen

"I think it was well known that if you were going to Josephines you had to get dressed up as if you were going to a wedding.

"I used to say that anyone who was anyone used to come into Josephine's. Anyone that used to play The Fiesta or Sheffield City Hall all came into us afterwards: Johnny Mathis, Tommy Cooper, Ronnie Corbett, Ronnie Barker – you name them and they were there.

"When we used to have the Snooker Ball [which welcomed the stars of the World Snooker Championships on their annual Sheffield visit which started in the late 1970s] we'd have the likes of James Hunt the racing driver turning up.

"If you wanted to book to get into the restaurant you'd have to book three or four weeks in advance. It was the best restaurant in town bar none."

You didn't dress down at Josephine's – dress codes were there to be stuck to and gents with long hair were sent packing.

Sheffield wrestling star Alan Kilby was a regular doorman.

★John Turnball

London Road's Tiffany's was another hotspot. John Turnball remembers the former Locarno fondly.

"Thursday and Sunday nights were really good. It was full of really fashionable people with all the men walking endlessly round the crowd of dancing women."

★Julie Wilson

"I had two 18th birthday parties. I had a family 18th birthday party in the Dial House WMC and then Josephine's put an 18th birthday on for me."

★A PASSPORT TO GLITZ

Peter McNerney: "You knew you'd made it in Sheffield when you acquired a Josephine's Gold Card. It was a passport to glitz and glamour. Well, more of a passport to the front of the queue. It was an invitation to those VIP Josie's birthday nights with the big buffet and the prawn mountain.

"I'm not quite sure who exactly qualified for a gold card but it sat in my wallet right alongside my credit cards, a vital part of the clubbing scene. It was of course important to look cool and trendy.

"That's why I went to Top Man and invested in a heavily discounted powder blue jacket. With the sleeves rolled up I resembled Crockett, or was it Tubbs, from Miami Vice. From the neck down at least.

"This special offer had struck a chord with the young single men of Sheffield because at least another half a dozen in Josie's were wearing the same jacket. It looked like the outside caterers had been brought in.

"But all this is the "high end" of Sheffield nightlife. Let's go back to the '70s and the Penthouse on Dixon Lane. How did they make the floor that sticky? And how come a bunch of sixth formers, most not 18, were able to book it for a disco party. And how come the endless stairs up to "The Penthouse" were so narrow. And what was that strange smell? Probably my Blue Stratos.

"Upstairs to The Penthouse, downstairs to the Limit. Ah, the "Lim". Down Lim as it was called. Don't pogo too high otherwise you'll hit the ceiling. All those plastic tables and chairs and a very small hatch where you'd get a re-heated burger. Was that part of the licensing restrictions? They had to serve food. Although I never met anyone who went to the Limit for a meal.

"So there we all were, mainly wearing black and posing on the edge of the dance floor not being able to say a word to anyone because it was too loud. Not being the Brad Pitt type the girls tended to look through me to my blond slim chum.

"But even in my late teens/early twenties I was old before my time. The Lim was too loud. Maxie's too vulgar. The Penthouse too grubby. I was happy to slip into a casual safari suit and have a date at the Fiesta. You've not lived until you've chuckled at the warm up comic, eaten the chicken in a basket, swilled the Blue Nun and been entertained by The Barron Knights. Or was it the

★ "So there we all were, mainly wearing black and posing on the edge of the dance floor."

Peter McNerney

Grumbleweeds. When I win the lottery we'll open a new Fiesta. Bankrupt by Christmas but it'll be great while it lasts.

"Today's young people...they don't know what they missed. Although after reading this they're probably not in the slightest bit bothered.

"I'm sure it was more fun. But remember I was the one being driven home. And it's amazing how a lager and lime can dull the memory."

Left: Peter McNerney as he is now

Below: Have car, will party - Peter McNerney's first motor

Peter McNerney in the seventies

TRD 822H

★John Mitchell

John Mitchell of Sheffield's renowned Mitchells Wines was a big fan of the seventies and the variety it boasted. Working in the trade, he knew the scene rather better than most. He said: "When my 20 year old daughter says she's going down town it means West Street. It's a great boozer's street but all the bars seem to be aimed at university students or the 18 to 30s.

"Unlike my daughters options we had loads of booze runs in the 1970s: The Wicker, Fitzalan Square, High Street, The Moor, London Road, Queens Road, Division Street and West Street!

"Starting at The Wicker arches, Station Inn, Viaduct, Punchbowl, New White Lion, Big Gun, Black Lion on the corner of Nursery Street then cross over to the Golden Ball, Brown Cow, Bull and Oak. So that was 9 pints, a quick look at what was showing on the saucy poster at Studio 7, which was as far as porn went then.

"These pubs weren't full of young lads but had a great mix; working men with shoes shined and smart three piece suits with watch chains, looking smart and

out on the town. We were also suited and booted because you wouldn't have got into a club later if you weren't."

John Mitchell today

John Mitchell on a pub crawl around The Moor:
"This was the crawl that got better as the night went on...
"It started at The Albert on Barkers Pool, which was okay but nothing special. Then the Barleycorn on Cambridge Street, the pits! My dad used to joke that he'd met my mum there. Its clientele included a few prostitutes; later it became Henry's. On to The Moor and The Nelson – once known as Fanny's, after the landlady.

"Then The Pump Tavern, known as Auntie Pump, after another post war landlady of the traditional mould (Mrs Jenkins, Nursery Tavern, Ecky Road).

"From there it was on to the best club for us, The Penny Farthing

next to the Hofbrauhaus.

"Hofbrauhaus was ace... it was also good for the stripper on a Saturday lunchtime on the way to Hillsborough. While at Hillsborough, don't forget, The Ozzie owners club and 'Christies'.

"Dave Baldwin, who owns The Omega on Psalter Lane, ran this. "The Penny Farthing was frequented by all the football players. My pal Len Badger, Sheffield United and England player, was a regular. He went on after football to have The Sidings at Dronfield, The Peacock at Barlow and the Fox & Goose near Chesterfield.

"When the club closed at 2am the food option was The Shapla on Cumberland Street - with a kitchen inspection before eating. However, when in The Moor vicinity, when we didn't go clubbing, it was always The Venus Steak House, brilliant steaks. Owned by a Cypriot family.

"One of my favourite venues was the Genevieve Club, Charter Square, owned by Max Omare, and his partner the lovely blond. He drove a yellow Rolls Royce. This club was advertised on TV as the 'nice club for nice people' but it wasn't a gay club, it was just a silly catchphrase. We went mostly into the small club upstairs which was the Mona Lisa.

"The walls were covered in very tasty pictures of nude women, a great little club.

"Faces night club on Charles Street was owned by a lady called Elaine and her brother.

"Turn Ups was another night spot at Nether Edge. This was owned by Les Vicars before he moved to Fannys (at Owler Bar)."

John Mitchell in 1971 with Sheffield model Christine Owen (later to become Christine Crapper)

SHOW ME THE WAY TO CHART SUCCESS

Sheffield music didn't have the best of times in the seventies and it's fair to say the charts weren't unduly bothered.

There were more than a few points in the era that the top twenty could have benefitted from a helping hand.

The first hit of the decade was Rolf Harris – he stayed at the number one spot for most of January 1970 with 'Two Little Boys'.

He was still hanging around in the top twenty in March.

Joe Cocker, Sheffield's favourite son and one of music's most enduring characters, didn't have the best of decades.

His last British chart flourish at that point was in 1969 with 'Delta Lady'.

Things he'd probably rather forget in the 1970s would have to include the occasion when he was given 48 hours to leave

★ **Things he'd probably rather forget in the 1970s would have to include the occasion when he was given 48 hours to leave Australia after he, and six members of his entourage, were arrested for possession of marijuana. The following day, assault charges were laid at his door after a brawl at the hotel.**

★

Australia after he, and six members of his entourage, were arrested for possession of marijuana.

The following day, assault charges were laid at his door after a brawl at the hotel.

The Australian Federal Police had had enough by that stage and sent him packing.

A year later he hid himself away in a remote cottage on Bodmin Moor for nine weeks.

Tony Christie was the city's biggest chart star of the early seventies, notching up three top forty singles.

'I Did What I Did For Maria' reached No. 2, 'Is This The Way to Amarillo' peaked at No. 18 and his 'Avenues and Alleyways' just snuck in at No. 37.

He spent much of the rest of the decade on the cabaret circuit, including headline appearances at the city's own Club Fiesta.

**Left:
Tony Christie –
the only local
artist to make a
serious dent in
the pop charts
in the 1970s**

Twenty years at the top... a Eurostar supreme

DAVE BERRY

The eternal
handyman
of pop
is the
godfather
of punk

Berry:
'On stage
I'm mean
and
wild'

Family man — Berry with wife and daughter

NEW wave music owes more than a small debt to 'sixties star Dave "Boots" Berry. It was the sinister, almost evil presence of Berry, which gave Punk rockers the gloves, scarves, boots, chains, leather gear and all-black rebel image.

Berry, now 35, is Holland's top solo singer. He is a big name in Belgium and at £1,500 a week is a European all-round rock star. Bad boy Berry, the Woodhouse-born son of a retired property repairer, is big business. And he's got style.

Dave, whose latest single, "Night of the Fly", is due out soon, is riding on the crest of success with a fat £25,000 record contract.

Twenty trend-setting years at the top and Dave still hasn't a speck of grey in his mop of black hair. And today's

Report by
Trevor
Reynolds

Dave Berry visits a fan in hospital

★Nigel Lockwood

"New Year's Day, 1978, the Heavy Metal Kids played Top Rank in Sheffield [featuring future Auf Wiedersehen Pet star Gary Holton on vocals].

"They all turned up at my house wanting to crash. It was 3.30am and they were all parked outside.

"I'd got my mum and dad asleep in the house."

Sheffield's most notable involvement in the country's glam rock scene, that dominated the charts from the early seventies, was probably drummer Pete Gill.

The city-based musician ended up playing for Gary Glitter at the height of his UK fame in the seventies – including two sell out nights at Sheffield City Hall.

Pete Gill: "I'd never played the City Hall before and in those days, with that sort of band, you needed an escort into the show and out again. The reaction to the show was unbelievable. I always remember being impressed with the dressing rooms, even though they were the old fashioned dressing rooms and, at that time, peo-ple could actually sit behind the stage, so we'd got another 200 or so people behind us, which was very unusual.

"I also liked the security with their dark red blazers – job-sworths, but great. I used to get along with them really well."

Pete Gill said he'd probably have liked to take the band on a sightseeing tour of Sheffield at the time but admitted things would have simply got out of hand.

He said: "Because of the popularity of the band, wherever you went you got mobbed. So if we went in a club you'd never be left alone. VIP areas, in those days, were very few and far between."

★ **"In those days, with that sort of band, you needed an escort into the show and out again..."**

Pete Gill

Popular Sheffield act The Negatives

Swallows were the tattoo of choice in the 1970s... even for the ladies. Pic shows local tattooist John Quinlan in action with a regular in 1972

Below: Artery perform in Weston Park

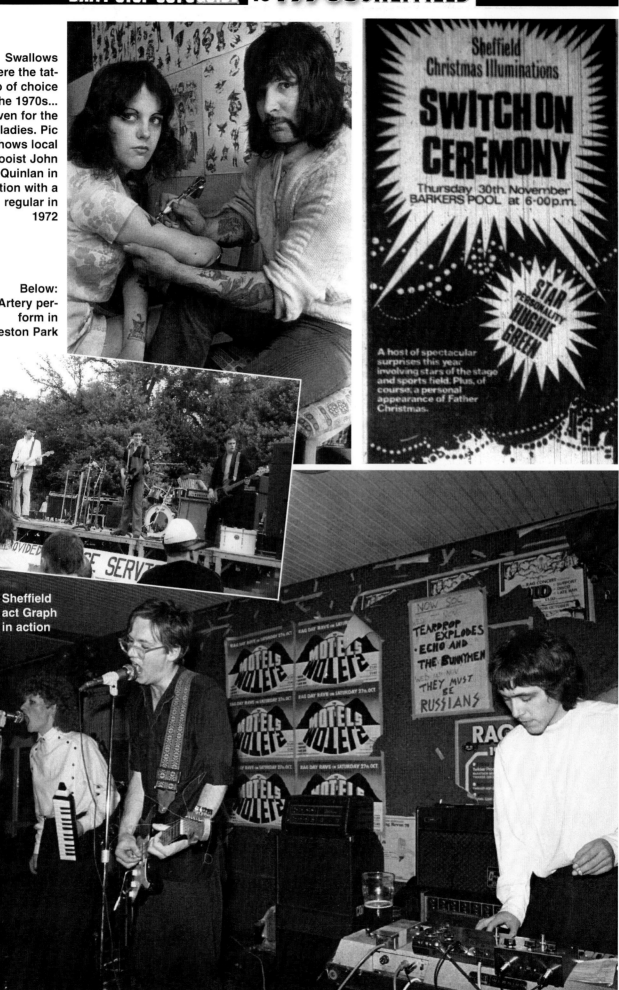

Sheffield act Graph in action

The Extras at London's Marquee

Sheffield's first ever hit maker, Jimmy Crawford, who scored a No. 49 hit in June 1961 with 'Love Or Money' and a No.18 with 'I Love How You Love Me', kept gigging throughout the 1970s as well as popping up on the likes of TV shows 'Opportunity Knocks' and 'New Faces'.

Sheffield band, The Extras, had a massive following in the mid to late seventies and were tipped for greatness but, unfortunately, it never happened, despite a recording contract being waved under their noses.

The Push, fronted by Ray Ashcroft, who later made his name as a soap actor in 'The

Bill' and 'Emmerdale', also had a big following and were one of the first acts to headline at legendary West Street venue The Limit.

Bizarrely, whilst the whole country was sticking a safety pin through its nose, Sheffield started hitting the big time with big hair and heavy metal in the shape of Def Leppard.

Their roots can be traced back to 1975 when 15-year-old Rick Savage signed schoolboy forms with Sheffield United (despite being a massive Sheffield Wednesday fan).

He soon got disillusioned and decided he'd rather form a band with friend Tony Kenning

and promptly ordered a guitar from his mother's catalogue.

By November 1977 the band were going under the name of Def Leppard and were fronted by Joe Elliot; practicing in a run-down spoon factory near Sheffield United.

Their first real concert was on July 18, 1978, at Westfield School in the Mosborough area.

A poster advertising The Extras at London's Marquee following the band's move to the capital

A very young Phil Oakey with Human League

One of the maddest line-ups in music history followed a few weeks later when they supported another fledgling act from the city, Human League, at West Street's Limit venue.

Their 'Def Leppard EP' was released in early 1979 on their own Bludgeon Riffola label.

It sold out quickly due to sessions on Radio Hallam and John Peel and the buzz attracted the attention of Phonogram Records. The Def Leppard buzz is still growing, over three decades on.

John Peel also played his own part in the rise of the Human League. He was a big fan of the band's 1978 release, 'Being Boiled', and championed it.

By March 1979 Human League were the cover stars of NME and at the forefront of the Sheffield electronic explosion that would firmly put the city on the national and international musical map within months.

The aftermath of a Bay City Rollers gig at Sheffield City Hall

VIRGIN, BRADLEY'S AND OTHER PURVEYORS OF QUALITY TUNES

CANN
SHEFFIELD'S
LEADING
RECORD
CASSETTE & CARTRIDGE
SHOP

Bigger and better than ever before.

Left:
Inside Philip
Cann on
Chapel Walk

Bradley's Records on Fargate

FACES

Sheffield teddy boys mark the death of Elvis Presley

Right:
A very young Paul Weller at a Jam signing session at Revolution Records at Castle Market in July 1977 Left to right: Revolution regular Mick Denton, Pete the shop owner and Paul Weller

The seventies were marked by some pretty jaw-dropping developments in music and fashion. Many shops and their staff found it hard to keep up and adapt.

Philip Cann on Chapel Walk found it harder than most – the management insisted pop fans were greeted with the dulcet tones of classical music whenever they entered.

Sheryl Littlewood, who worked there at the time, said: "The management were very old school. I remember my boss, Mrs Hinch, she was like an old school ma'am.

"We weren't even allowed to talk to our fellow shop assistants!

"We had to play classical music all the time, but on Mrs Hinch's day off we went mad and played pop records."

Things were rather different at the bottom of The Moor at Virgin.

It was managed by one Barry Everard (who you'll now find running the revered Record Collector outlet in Broomhill – he has been up there since the late seventies).

He landed the Virgin job thanks to him being a walking, talking encyclopedia of music – a fact that came to light when he was standing in the Virgin queue one day.

Whilst record staff stood dumbfounded at customer questions regarding particular artists Barry just rolled the answers off the top of his head.

Virgin were that impressed they gave him a job.

Chris Wintle: "Virgin was wonderful. It had two listening booths at the bottom of the shop.

Pistols' secret thanks

PUNK ROCK stars the Sex Pistols shot into Sheffield on a secret visit to thank local record shops for stocking their controversial Number One album.

Guitarist Steve Jones and drummer Paul Cook — lead singer Johnny Rotten couldn't be found in London — slipped into the city virtually unnoticed yesterday.

"We just came up here on the train because of the trouble the shops have been going to with the album — and to have a bit of fun," said Cook.

Their first L.P. — banned by major stores like Boots, W. H. Smith and Woolworth — caused a storm of fury because of a swear word in its title. Shopkeepers selling it have been charged under Victorian laws about indecent advertising.

The Sex Pistols have played in Sheffield once, at the Black Swan pub, since closed down, with another group who have now become punk stars — the Clash.

"About ten people turned up then," said Cook to the 30-odd punks who's heard by word of mouth about the secret visit to Sheffield. "We'd like to play here again — but they just won't let us. The councils and the law won't let us play anywhere."

The two Pistols left Sheffield last night for Manchester.

Kung Fu attacks hit the playground

KUNG FU violence is spreading to the playgrounds of London schools, it was claimed today.

Mr. Charles Paley-Phillips, a Conservative member of Waltham Forest Council, said parents and teachers had complained about children being attacked "in Kung Fu style with kicks and chops."

He said: "This is extremely dangerous. Someone will soon be seriously injured." Kung Fu was an art that needed special training.

He called for TV warnings about the dangers, and is to take the matter up with education chiefs.

52

"It was full of hippies mainly. I bought my first album from there: a country rock album by Poco called 'A Good Feeling To Know'. It was full price at £1.99."

The shop was famed for the aircraft seats you sat in to hear music.

Future Iron Maiden singer and pilot Bruce Dickinson was hardly out of them under Barry Everard's watch.

Chris Twiby: "Virgin had a healthy air of menace about it. It was very dark but stylish. I remember it had very early copies of the Ramones first album before anyone else. It used to have some really cutting edge stuff in. It always seem to have a bizarre mix of hippies and punks standing around looking as though they owned the place."

Just up the road was the legendary Violet Mays; Wilson Pecks lived on Leopold Street.

Left: Clearing up the aftermath of soccer violence in 1973 in The Claymore

★Nigel Lockwood

Nigel Lockwood on Revolution Records that used to reside at Castle Market: "They always had a list on the wall of the releases that were due out the following week. They always had a punk list as well."

★Doug Huntingdon

"I worked in the melting department at Firth Brown on Saville Street. It was a hard job, a tough job, but we made up for it when we went out. We went out night clubbing every night. I used to sometimes get in at 3 O'clock in a morning and I was up at 5, to get to work. We used to drink like fish then, 8 or 10 pints."

Hosts of Arundel Gate's Claymore – Jean and Terry Cole in 1976

Above and left: The thriving Working Men's Club scene of the seventies

★ TALES FROM TIVOLI BAR IN FITZALAN SQUARE

The long gone Tivoli venue used to sit under The Marples in Fitzalan Square.

Martin Bellamy, who was a bouncer at Wapentake Bar at the time, was persuaded to come and help out. He said: "The only security they'd got was a guy called Joe – a commissionaire type who normally worked up at the Nat West Bank. He wore this jacket with medals and sergeant stripes.

"I got talking to him and it turned out he was a Burma veteran and boy could he move when he had to.

"He used to stand on the door with a little bag taking money.

"In the summer, when it was full, they used to open the back door and they used to need two doorman on the back door to ensure nobody else came in. Me and a guy called Dave Smith did it. We made sure people did come in and we made £30 a night each! We used to ram the place."

Though Tivoli Bar was only short-lived it led to Martin getting the chance to police the city's biggest club of the era and learning the secret code given out by the DJ to point security to trouble spots whilst not alerting customers to any fracas.

He said: "One night the guy that used to organise our Tivoli football team said 'I've heard they're looking for doormen on Saturdays at the Top Rank'.

"He said 'they're wanting as many people as possible' and I thought 'that's a bit strange – are they having a mass clear-out?'

"Well I was sat in the office at Top Rank with the manager and he said 'well what you'll hear is seven things from the DJ.

You'll hear 'gentlemen bar number one, or number two and so on'. Well 'bar number one' is the dance floor near the stage, bar number two' is the top dance floor and so on.

"And just as he finished this we heard 'gentleman bar number one'. This manager-type immediately jumps up and I followed him out and we walked straight out onto the stage.

"It was all kicking off and I saw other colleagues that had come up from the Wapentake with me and we all dived in."

★Chris Wintle

Chris Wintle on Violet May's: "I heard all these stories about getting shouted at if you didn't buy anything!"

Violet May's

Wilson Peck – purveyors of fine tunes and Sheffield City Hall tickets

PENNY FARTHING
AND A ROLLICKING BAVARIAN STYLE KNEES UP NEXT DOOR

T he Penny Farthing was definitely one of the most revered nightclubs of the era. It considered itself a notch above most other places.

Hofbrauhaus next door was a rather different animal.

We weren't mentioning the war anymore and now everyone wanted to drink German-style.

Eyre Street lapped it up and the people came from miles around for "a really rollicking Bavarian style night out" and the beer came direct from Germany.

Hofbrauhaus offered its own in-house Oompah band and other drinking-marathon-style entertainment.

There was even a yearly Miss Hofbrau competition.

Left:
Raising
a stein to
life at
Hofbrauhaus

CHAPTER EIGHT

Right: Orrett and Jacqueline Hanson on their wedding night... At Hofbrauhaus

The Hofbrauhaus entrance

Below: Hofbrauhaus staff

Orrett Hanson had one of the fastest rises through the ranks in the history of seventies nightlife.

He started as a glass collector just a few weeks after opening in 1973. He was then duly promoted to bouncer, head doorman and ended up as bar manager for the lifetime of the venue and onwards as it became Dingwells in the 1980s.

His love of the place was as strong as any marriage – he even wed one of the regulars, Jacqueline, and they're still together over three decades on.

The place was a massive success from the day it opened.

Orrett Hanson: "We'd have up to 900 people in there. I used to book the parties in and I'd allocate them to their seats on arrival.

"We'd have anything up to 100 people in any one party.

"The entertainment was the Oompah band with a DJ in-between. The Oompah band would come on twice a night and everyone would dance on the tables.

"The DJ would play Tamla Motown and disco music whilst the band stuck to German music. The band went down well – it was a real novelty.

"Thursday, Friday and Saturday were our big nights – the rest of the week was steady. Many people would go straight to the Penny Farthing next door afterwards."

Coaches would arrive from all around the region: parties from Leeds, Bradford and Nottingham would be common. It was part of the Hofbrauhaus chain, with others in Hull, Blackpool and other Stein swilling strongholds.

Orrett's meeting with his future wife wasn't quite Mills and Boon – he helped pick her up off the floor of the Hofbrauhaus after she'd had too much to drink apparently – but they're still going strong and they've probably outlasted half the marriages from the era.

Above: Orrett Hanson (right) in residence at Hofbrauhaus

Right: Orrett Hanson and lady friends at Hofbrauhaus

Hofbrauhaus staff including Jacqueline Hanson (third from left)

★ "We had another incident where the wife of one of the managers was in the office and she spotted her husband watching the strippers. She played hell with him and proceeded to get on the stage and started stripping herself. I had to go up and drag her off."

Orrett Hanson

Doorman Stuart Smith said they ended up having to ban stag parties as things regularly got out of hand.

He said: "When we got trouble we really got it. If you came with a party of 25 you got in cheaper, but parties regularly fought each other. We ended up stopping stag parties and only allowed mixed parties."

Hofbrauhaus entertainment wasn't always based on the picture postcard feel of the sweeping Bavarian Alps.

Tastes change; by the mid to late seventies the Oompah band had begun to fall out of favour.

Dinner times offered strippers, topless go-go dancers, free booze and sausage and mash for just 27p.

Orrett Hanson: "We weren't getting the custom and the novelty had worn off a bit. The strippers went on for nearly three years. It was only 5p to get in. It was very popular for the first 18 months. All the firms used to come in their dinner hour.

"We had an incident one dinner time when a guy was watching a stripper and his wife turned up unannounced and threw beer all over him.

"We had another incident where the wife of one of the managers was in the office and she spotted her husband watching the strippers. She played hell with him and proceeded to get on the stage and started stripping herself. I had to go up and drag her off."

A fight breaks out at Hofbrauhaus

Jackie Stanley's 20th birthday party at Hofbrauhaus in 1975

Jackie Stanley gets to conduct the band as part of her birthday celebrations

Right: Inside Scamps in 1977

Below: The entrance to Scamps

By 1977 the Penny Farthing next door had reinvented itself as the popular Scamps. Marked by images of sultry looking ladies at the entrance and elaborate Victorian-style mirrors inside (complete with images of yet more ladies – this time in Victorian underwear).

The venue didn't appeal to John Goodwin of The Star at the time. He gave it a right slating and left no stone unturned in his quest to find problems.

The cloakroom attendant was the first to get it in the neck.

"We arrived in the club early and found the cloakroom attendant unwilling to stay at her station. The disc jockey had to interrupt records to call her over from the buffet bar."

Then he had a go at the temperature.

"Early in the evening, when few people were in the club, it was uncomfortably cold".

Sounds as though you shot yourself in the foot John – you shouldn't have been in such a hurry to hang up your coat.

He had issues with the "obtrusive" bandits, advised people with claustrophobia to stay away because the dance floor got busy and didn't like the microwaved food, or the lack of starters and desserts.

Oh, and the price of the beer, at 41p a pint, was deemed "a little high".

A busy dance floor, dodgy microwave comfort food, expensive beer and pictures of girls seemed hallmarks of every successful club in the late seventies.

Kind of makes you wonder what Johnny boy was expecting that night. Thank god he didn't go for bangers and mash at Hofbrauhaus.

GET TOGETHER at

NURSES & STUDENTS PARTY NIGHT

TOMORROW NIGHT
AN-END-OF-TERM EXTRAVAGANZA FREE BUFFET
Super Fun Contests, Prizes and Surprises!
Friends welcome, too!

Scamps
EYRE STREET, SHEFFIELD.
Phone 28403.

MEET OUR SWINGING NEW D.J.
AFTER HIS SEASON IN PARIS
GARTH CAWOOD
MAKE A DATE FOR OUR NEW
WEDNESDAY SCENE
featuring LIVE MUSIC
EVERY WEDNESDAY.
OPEN 8 p.m. to 2 a.m.
MEMBERS' NOTICE.

PENNY FARTHING CLUB,
EYRE STREET, SHEFFIELD.

Inside the Penny Farthing

★Lynda Butterell

"In the 1970s, before Josephine's, Penny Farthing was the place to go. It was the most upmarket. All the footballers used to go. I had my hen party there."

★Denise Huntingdon

"Doug and me met at the Penny Farthing. It was brilliant. It was classed as being a bit better.

"It wasn't a very big place and they used to have some nights where they had local groups on. They also had student nights. I was training at the dental hospital at the time and used to get in cheap.

"We'd probably start our night at either Marples or The Claymore. You'd not be able to move in The Claymore normally. We'd sometimes go to The Mulberry Tavern nearby.

Above: Doug and Denise Huntingdon tie the knot

Left: Denise and Doug Huntington with elephant in more recent times

"Then it would be off to the Blue Bell before going to the Dove and Rainbow. The Stonehouse was a definite. Maybe the Three Tuns and The Museum. We'd normally go to The Buccaneer. We might go further up still – maybe

The Albert. It was great. All those pubs. If we were late we'd know exactly where to find everyone.

"I can say, hand on heart, that I never saw anyone taking any drugs. People were just happy to have a drink."

Doug Huntingdon

WEDDING PARADE

MR Chris Glosson, of Nethershire Lane, Shiregreen, and Miss Patricia Nolan, of Pyebank Drive, Pitsmoor, were married at Sheffield Register Office.

CORPORAL Stephen Gregory, of Idsworth Road, Firth Park, and Miss Roswitha Tabor, of Walsrode, West Germany, were married at Sheffield Register Office.

MR Colin Exley, of The Greenway, Carr Road, Deepcar, and Miss Angela Foster, of Manchester Road, Deepcar, were married at Sheffield Register Office.

MR Lawrence Cart, of Lowedges Road, Sheffield, and Mrs Valerie Furniss, of Fox Street, Pitsmoor, were married at Sheffield Register Office.

MR Graham Jenson, of Greystones Avenue, Sheffield, and Miss Pat Maxfield, of Sothall Green, Beighton, were married at Sheffield Register Office.

MR Mark Boulding, of Fisher Lane, Darnall, and Miss Valerie Wood, of Atkins Drive, Parson Cross, were married at Sheffield Register Office.

MR David Parkin, of Oak Park, Broomhill, and Miss Diane Sollitt, of Leighton Road, Gleadless, were married at Sheffield Register Office.

MR Alan Hope, of Sunningdale Mount, Ecclesall, and Miss Louise Birch, of Slayleigh Lane, Fulwood, were married at Sheffield Register Office.

MISS Margaret Anna Wnuk, of Coalbrook Road, Woodhouse Mill, and Mr Kevin Hicken, of Wayfield Close, Dronfield Woodhouse, were married at St James' Church, Woodhouse.

MRS Joy Goddard, of Catherine Road, Sheffield, and Mr Colin also of Catherine Road, were married at Sheffield Register Office.

MR J Walker, of Cantilupe Crescent, Aston, and Miss C Horne, also of Cantilupe Crescent, were married at Rotherham Register Office.

MR Graham Marples, of Wesley Avenue, Swallownest, and Miss Pauline Leedham, also of Wesley Avenue, Swallownest, were married at Rotherham Register Office.

A go go dancing competition in the Penny Farthing in 1970. Terry Steeples of the Black Swan is in the middle of the crowd wearing a dinner suit

Police patrol in Fitzalan Square

GONE TO THE DOGS

CHAPTER NINE

**Right:
A view over
Owlerton
Stadium**

An Owlerton
Stadium bar

Above: Owlerton Stadium's hare

Few venues have rivalled the staying power of Penistone Road's Owlerton Stadium, which first opened as a speedway track in 1929.

Greyhounds were introduced in 1932 and have been the operation's mainstay ever since.

Variety at the venue was at an all time high in the 1970s.

Swimming costume-clad beauty pageants, show jumping and football were just some of the events you could regularly see alongside greyhound racing, speedway and stock-cars.

Jon Carter took over the management of the venue in 1972 and has been a larger than life face there ever since.

"It only washed its face financially at that time but it was so much fun doing it", he said.

Owlerton Stadium might not have been achieving the profits it has in more recent years, but it was definitely one of the most popular after dark outings of the era.

The variety on offer was a prominent feature in The Reel Monty film – the early seventies Sheffield City Council promotional flick that went on to front The Full Monty and become one of the most watched films of its kind ever.

Jon Carter admits the track has had its fair share of ups

★Nigel Lockwood

"Speedway was massive in the 1970s. I used to go to all the Sheffield Tigers meetings – both home and away. Wrestling was massive. My favourite wrestler was Kendo Nagasaki."

★FROM TOP DOG TO ALL NIGHT HOT DOG

Bouncer Martin Bellamy: "The 24 hour Wimpy on Fargate was a real dirty stop out's place. There was one night in about 1971 when it was getting to about 2am when one of the staff asked me if I fancied doing four hours on the door.

"They said 'just stand there and you'll get a free breakfast'. So I used to stay there until 6am. There'd hardly be anybody in, but it was just a case of stopping drunks getting inside or getting rid of drunks – stuff like that. I then got my free meal with bent Frankfurters in the middle of it, or something like that."

and downs over the decades.

"There were plans for the stadium to be re-possessed and flattened. The space was to be used to build a venue for the World Student Games."

Owlerton Stadium hung on and gleaming new facilities like Don Valley Stadium and Ponds Forge were built to stage the games.

One of Owlerton Stadium's saviours – according to Jon – was one Margaret Thatcher.

"Her Sunday trading laws gave greyhound racing a real future. Up until that point we were only allowed to stage two meetings per week, but after that we could race whenever we liked", he said.

Things reached crisis point following the Hillsborough Disaster in 1989 – the council shut the stadium for six months until it met stringent new safety laws.

"It was an absolute nightmare of

a time for us – we ended up having to race from Nottingham for a period, despite the fact we'd never had more than a sprained ankle amongst the general public since the day the track opened.

"By this time we were looking at huge capital investment, or it was the end of the road for Owlerton Stadium."

The venue's saviour came in the shape of Sheffield entrepreneur Dave Allen, who was already renowned for his city-based Josephine's nightclub, that opened in Sheffield in 1976, and his expanding Napoleons Casino chain.

Jon Carter said: "Things never looked back after Dave Allen came in and started his multi-million pound reinvestment. He has completely revamped the place and introduced a whole new audience to greyhound racing."

★ **Variety at the venue was at an all time high in the 1970s. Swimming costume-clad beauty pageants, show jumping and football were just some of the events you could regularly see alongside greyhound racing, speedway and stock cars**

Max Omare was a true king of the clubs in the 1970s running everything from Shades on Ecclesall Road to Genevieve in Charter Square

CHAPTER TEN ★

GETTING SHIPWRECKED
AT THE BUCCANEER

The Buccaneer was already well into its stride in 1970 under the watchful eye of Olga Marshall, who went on to manage the Wapentake years later.

It was a series of theme bars attached to the Grand Hotel upstairs and owned by Trust House Forte.

She started there as a barmaid in 1964 and soon made it clear she wasn't happy with the way things operated.

Olga Marshall, who still lives in Sheffield, said: "We'd only got a jukebox so I spoke to the

★ **"My girlfriend cried her eyes out when The Buccaneer shut – she was absolutely gutted."**
Paul Smith

management company about getting a DJ in. They brought in a company called DRM, I think, who came along with flashing lights and the full set up but they just weren't what we wanted at all.

"I asked if I could sort something out myself and found George Webster, who was playing at the Canon Hall social club at Page Hall at the time. He started playing the kind of music my customers liked.

"We took more on our first night with George than The Buccaneer took on its average weekend."

The Buccaneer became one of the busiest and most popular venues in the city in the early seventies.

Olga herself rarely drank, didn't smoke and was already a mother of four in 1972.

Left: Olga Marshall in The Buccaneer

The Buccaneer in action

Olga Marshall and Buccaneer staff

Regular Peter Eales said: "There was nowhere else playing music like it in Sheffield. You went to The Buccaneer if you wanted to hear stuff that was different and wasn't mainstream.

"It had a real buzz about it. There were lots of different rooms but it was that dark you could never tell where you were anyway."

The Buccaneer shut its doors for the last time in 1973 after 1,979 days of custom.

Clive Porter just missed it: "I once went as far as the doorway of the Buccaneer but some of my bolder friends went in. Not long after that it closed, so I never actually got to go in.

"I did quite like The Museum in Orchard Square – it had a good jukebox. There was also The Albert at the top of Cambridge Street."

The Buccaneer sign still sits in Olga's garage in Gleadless along with one of the tables.

She wasn't out of work for long.

Olga was soon welcoming former Buccaneer punters in her new home, Wapentake Bar, sited five minutes up the road.

George Webster followed her before opening The Limit on West Street in 1978.

★Jon Downing

"In 1973 a group of us got together and started going to gigs at Sheffield City Hall (no other venues were coming on the radar at that time!) - and I managed to get to see Focus, Bowie (the Aladdin Sane tour), Genesis (twice - one with, one without Peter Gabriel) and Roxy Music.

"Early 1974 saw me attending Wizzard and Gong gigs there too. Before going into the City Hall, we'd pop down into the bowels of The Buccaneer and enjoy a pint or two, from plastic glasses - possibly the first pub in the world to use them?"

Buccaneer assistant manager Norman Coldwell (left) and DJs George Webster (middle) and Ian Roberts

AHOY THERE!!
come aboard
THE BUCCANEER BARS
LEOPOLD STREET
for a swinging swashbuckling Easter
4 BARS, CONTINUOUS DISCS NIGHTLY.
SAT. LUNCHTIME — Special disco show.
EASTER MONDAY — DISCO GO-GO GIRLS
WENCHES — Come in the gear and be MISS BUCCANEER.
ENTER THE YARD OF ALE COMPETITION.

All your favourite draught and bottled beers — served in the pleasant nautical atmosphere of the
CAPTAINS CABIN BAR
And lunch at the Captain's Cold Table – 45p
Choice of succulent pork, ham, tongue, beef, salads, pickles, fresh bread and butter.
Grand Hotel Building, Leopold St. — above Buccaneer Bar

Captain's Cabin Bar re-launch ceremony

★Tony Beesley

"Sheffield back in the seventies? It's all a mix of hazy memories for me. I was far too young to have experienced much of the fondly remembered '70s nightlife of the city: I used to hear my brothers talk of drunken nights out at the Fiesta, Bierkeller and the like, but my years of night life fun would have to wait until almost the very end of the decade with my teenage introduction to punk rock in the city.

"The first time I walked up the Top Rank ramp/bridge over the subway, I was in awe. There were punks all over the place with as many variations of hair colour that I could possibly imagine. "The clothes were not the uniform of leather jackets and mohawk that is now widely - and wrongly - thought of as the typical punk visual...or maybe that is the typical, but these guys were not!

"There were bandsmen's jackets, guardsmen's jackets, long macs of every colour, plastic macs, zip jackets, zip trousers, baggy mohair jumpers of all colours, bleached hair, multi coloured hair. shaved hair, Mick Jones lookalikes. Johnny Thunders look-alikes, panda eyed punk girls wearing hardly anything with torn fishnets, torn T-shirts - and me in my plastic trousers and Buzzcocks shirt thinking I looked cool and different...ummm. I might have done back in Rawmarsh but stood here with my mini-punk kid mates we felt positively unnoticeable! That night was to see The Stranglers: many more punk nights at the Top Rank were to come."

PENTHOUSE, WAPENTAKE

AND GIGS AT SHEFFIELD CITY HALL

Peter Stringfellow's Penthouse was the Sheffield-born night-club owner's first foray into a real business with an alcohol licence.

The year was 1969.

It should, on the face of it, been a licence to print money.

He'd got an enviable rapport with major bands, having promoted everyone from The Beatles to Jimi Hendrix in the past. He'd built up a big following via earlier successes at his Mojo and Down Broadway venues in Sheffield.

Peter Stringfellow ended up selling The Penthouse business within months of opening.

It was, in his eyes, a disaster.

Situated on Dixon Lane, the club was at the top of flight after flight of stairs – hence the name, The Penthouse.

The youngsters that had been his coffee-supping bread and butter at earlier ventures were now growing up and turning into

a rather more potent mix – young adults with a thirst for alcohol.

And they were soon being pushed out by a new crowd that headed to The Penthouse after a night's partying on Sheffield's rowdy West Street.

Peter Stringfellow: "Down Broadway had been similar to the Mojo in that the crowd were young and didn't drink. I hoped they would follow me to The Penthouse, but instead I got an entirely different crowd. Many of them had grown up in a Working Men's Club environment and were used to drinking, but they hadn't experienced drinking,

dancing and live music. I began attracting the kind of clientele I should have never let in the place."

Like his previous two clubs, murals adorned the walls: Greek and Roman ones on the club itself whilst female dancing figures worked their way up the sides of the stairs.

Live music consisted of acts like Alan Bown Set who had been favourites at the Mojo.

Peter Stringfellow's mother regularly ran the box office with security provided by 'Big' Brian Turner and others.

Fighting became a consistent problem in the early days and Peter Stringfellow didn't hang around for long – he soon sold up, but The Penthouse carried on regardless.

The venue ended up as a hard drinking rock club for most of the seventies – definitely not the vision of Peter Stringfellow.

Hen party nights, beat the clock nights – it was the second home for party animals everywhere.

★WAPENTAKE BAR

Wapentake Bar entrance

Another venue that set out with rather a different image than the one it ended up with was Wapentake Bar – the operation under Charter Square's Grosvenor Hotel owned by Trust House Forte.

It was the second bar venture for former Buccaneer Bar manager Olga Marshall.

She begrudgingly toed the company line for the first few months, with less of a rock outlook, but by the mid-seventies the volume was firmly stuck at 11.

George "Buccaneer" Webster – Olga's DJ from the Buccaneer – was soon attracting a new crowd to Wapentake Bar.

Management at the Grosvenor House Hotel were actually eager to do their bit to help wel-

★Jackie Capper

"I first went into Wapentake when I was 14. I told my mum I was going to see Queen at the City Hall."

come their new rock crowd.

"The hotel manager, Mr Tallis, suggested we ought to have a party for the rockers and he offered to lay on some jelly," said Olga.

"I told him not to be so stupid. He did take his suit off one night, came down in a T-shirt and told me: 'Your crowd are actually alright to talk to.' I'm not quite sure what he expected!"

As with The Buccaneer, as the takings increased, interference from the hotel upstairs decreased.

Wapentake Bar regulars

Wapentake DJs and future Limit people George Webster (left) and Paul Unwin

The Penthouse.
DIXON LANE SHEFFIELD TELE 26871.
VALUE TICKET
FOR ALL THE BEST SOUNDS OF
TODAY, TOMORROW AND YESTERYEAR,

MONDAY
Free Admission With This Ticket Till 10·30pm
Normal Admission 50p..25p Drinks All Night

TUESDAY
Closed Except For Private Hire
Private Hire Available Most Nights Of The Week
From only £15·00.

WEDNESDAY
Free Admission With This Ticket Till 10·30pm
Normal Admission 50p 25p Drinks All Night

THURSDAY
HEN PARTY NITE One Free Round Of Drinks Given to
Hen Party Of 6 Or More Up To The Value Of
£3·00 Before 10·30pm
Free admission with this ticket
Normal admission 50p

FRIDAY
BEAT THE CLOCK NIGHT
40p Admission Till 10·30 70p Admission After
Plus 25p Drinks Till 10·30pm

SATURDAY
80p Admission 25p Drinks Till 10·30pm.
Management Reserve The Right To Refuse Admission And
Alter Or Withdraw This Ticket Without Prior Notice

The Penthouse✱✱
VALUE TICKET
MONDAY
18p DRINKS ALL NIGHT
Free with this ticket till 10pm
Normal charge 45p
18p Drinks, Whisky, Gin, Bacardi, Brandy, Pints
Lager, Beer etc.

TUESDAY
✰ OPEN FOR PRIVATE HIRE ✰
(See Manager)

WEDNESDAY
18p Drinks All Night
Free with ticket till 10pm
Normal charge 45p

THURSDAY
Free all night with ticket
45p Normal Admission
'HEN PARTY NIGHT'

FRIDAY
30p before 10·30
18p DRINKS before 10·30pm
Admission after 10·30 65p

SATURDAY
18p DRINKS Before 10·30pm
ADMISSION 75p

RETAIN THIS TICKET NIGHTLY

The Penthouse.
DIXON LANE SHEFFIELD TELE 26871.
VALUE TICKET.
FOR ALL THE BEST SOUNDS OF
TODAY, TOMORROW AND YESTERYEAR,

MONDAY
Free Admission With This Ticket Till 10·30pm
Normal Admission 50p..25p Drinks All Night

TUESDAY
Closed Except For Private Hire
Private Hire Available Most Nights Of The Week
From only £15·00.

WEDNESDAY
Free Admission With This Ticket Till 10·30pm
Normal Admission 50p 25p Drinks All Night

THURSDAY
HEN PARTY NITE One Free Round Of Drinks Given to
Hen Party Of 6 Or More Up To The Value Of
£3·00 Before 10·30pm
Free admission with this ticket
Normal admission 50p

FRIDAY
BEAT THE CLOCK NIGHT
40p Admission Till 10·30 70p Admission After
Plus 25p Drinks Till 10·30pm

SATURDAY
80p Admission 25p Drinks Till 10·30pm.
Management Reserve The Right To Refuse Admission And
Alter Or Withdraw This Ticket Without Prior Notice

Right: Olga Marshall in residence at the Wapentake Bar

Few people would ever associate the, then, swish Grosvenor House Hotel (the hotel presently awaits demolition) on Charter Square roundabout in the city centre as the owners of the Wapentake. It probably worked better that way: only the management and a few others knew the two were inherently linked; it would have done little for the street cred of either operation had the situation been otherwise.

Wapentake Bar had its own entrance out of view of the hotel. You had to descend a flight of stairs before you got so much as a sniff of the action.

The Wapentake
Wellington Street
We have now opened our superb
TAKE AWAY SERVICE
Crusties and Breadcakes (with delicious fillings)
Hot Pies and Sausage Rolls,
Soup and Mushy Peas.
OPEN 6 DAYS A WEEK
9.30 a.m. TILL 2.30 p.m.
N.B. Full bar facilities and sit-down Restaurant
downstairs as usual.
TELEPHONE 20041, ext. 100
MANAGERESS, Mrs. O. MARSHALL.

Décor was – at best – basic; it had a very low ceiling and the place was sweaty and dark.

The punters couldn't have been happier and the place was soon running seven nights a week and was also promoting regular gigs - Def Leppard played one of their first ever outings down there. The bar soon became legendary on the UK rock scene.

It was also the training ground for future Limit DJ Paul Unwin, who started working for George Webster at the Wapentake.

There was rarely trouble, despite the venue's appeal to biker gangs whom the firm hand of Olga Marshall always managed to control – and it was always renowned for its almost 'family atmosphere'.

Ian Cheetham: "Wapentake Bar became an absolute magnet for rockers – if you were in Sheffield you had to go to The Wap. I was a punter there for nearly two decades and nobody could believe it was run by this smartly dressed mother of four who took no nonsense from anyone – Hells Angels or anyone."

Below: DJ Paul Unwin

Bottom: Mick Bailey (wearing hat) of Bailey Brothers fame with a very young Def Leppard

Bailey Brothers as they are today

★Dez Bailey

"This is where we first saw a very young Def Leppard performing UFO and Thin Lizzy covers. The ceiling was way too low to get a good sound but Leppard, even then, had a charm and energy about them.

We played with them eventually and were really pleased for them when things finally came together. No band in the world deserves to be successful more than our local heroes, especially after all the stuff they have been through. I can remember the famous football game in the corner which an old friend of ours, Frank Cross, would be on all night. He later went on to have one in his house complete with floodlights and juke box.

"You had to queue right down the road to get in the Wap, sometimes you would leg it to the Nelson hoping the queue would have diminished when you got back. The music was a bit dated but the scene was really cool and friendly. Olga ran a really good business there and should be applauded as the Grosvenor House Hotel owners didn't really want a rock pub but loved the takings."

Why did the fans queue all night?

THE queue — and the end is "out of sight"! Just part of today's crush for tickets.

ANSWER: THEY WANT TO SEE LED ZEPPELIN

LED ZEPPELIN MANIA hit Sheffield today! And the fans were showing their devotion to the pop group two months before they are even due to arrive in the city.

To make sure of a ticket for Zeppelin's City Hall concert on January 2 some fans queued all night in the cold and rain outside Wilson Peck's in Leopold Street.

By the time the doors opened at 9 a.m. this morning the queue had stretched right round into Barkers Pool and alongside the Grand Hotel building.

First fan on the scene was Robert Ramsain, aged 16, from Montague Street, Doncaster, who arrived at 10.45 last night.

"I wanted to make sure that I got a really good seat and the only way to do that is to get here early." he said.

He arrived with his friend, Robert Cottrell, also 16, and from Wheatley Hills, Doncaster. The lads braved the elements on one of the worst nights since last winter with a plastic bag to help keep them dry.

For their efforts they were rewarded with a free copy of the group's latest album by Wilson Peck's.

"Anyone who stayed out that long especially last night, deserves it," said the assistant general manager, Mr. P. Rowan.

What is so special about Led Zeppelin?

"They are the best rock band in the world," said Colin Coeuer, aged 17.

who has been an ardent fan of the group for some time. He and his three friends arrived early this morning from Pontefract armed with folding chairs, flasks, sandwiches and warm clothing.

Further along the queue was a devoted mum chasing a ticket for her schoolboy son. "He couldn't come because he had to go to school so I'm standing in for him. My friends all think I'm mad," she said.

Tickets, priced at £1, were being limited to two a person to stop black market dealings.

Far left: Fancy dress night promotion at the Wapentake bar

Right:
Mott The
Hoople at
Sheffield City
Hall

Far right:
Clive
Porter in
the 1970s

Whilst the Top Rank was the place for rising stars of the punk rock world, Sheffield City Hall was the place for rock throughout the era. Gigs were relentless.

Clive Porter: "I often think about all the artists that I didn't see – most notably David Bowie and Pink Floyd.

Below:
Mick Ronson
at Sheffield
City Hall –
April 29, 1974

"One of the first bands I did see there was Genesis – I still have the ticket stub. They were bottom of the bill with Lindisfarne and Van der Graaf Generator. I was only 14."

★Chris Wintle

Below right:
Mick Ronson
leaving
Sheffield City
Hall's stage
door – April
29, 1974

I remember Queen supporting Mott The Hoople. You just knew they were going to be massive – they were fantastic. I remember them doing Brighton Rock – I'd already heard the hype but they were worth even more than that."

David Bowie and The Spiders From Mars at Sheffield City Hall – June 6, 1973

Left:
Lou Reed at
Sheffield City
Hall –
September
29, 1973

★Denise Huntingdon

"Barley wine was the main one for women. Never liked the taste but it used to be a good one for a good night. I used to go a lot to Shades cause that were more student, mainly on Wednesday nights."

Left:
Brian Eno
at Sheffield
City Hall –
February
15, 1973

Far left:
A campaign
to save the
Lyceum
Theatre

Left:
The Lyceum
theatre at the
time of the
campaign

CITY HALL
SHEFFIELD

Wilson Peck Ltd.
Booking Agent:

STALLS
£1.75
INCLUDING VAT

M 11

DOOR E

Wednes.
Mar. 16
7.30 p.m.
TO BE GIVEN UP

CITY (OVAL) HALL
SHEFFIELD

Kennedy Street Ents. Ltd.
presents
GRAHAM PARKER and
The Rumour in concert

STALLS
£1.75
INCLUDING VAT

M 11

DOOR E

WED

MAR

16

7.30

BLACK SWAN

Snig Hill, Sheffield 3
Phone : 20526

Manager : Bob Rooney

on Tuesday, 27th April, 1976
T.V. and Recording Star
Gerry and the Pacemakers

Cover charge 55p
Doors open 8 p.m.

Management reserve the right to refuse admission.

CITY (OVAL) HALL
SHEFFIELD

Mel Bush
presents

QUEEN
+ SUPPORT

GRAND CIRCLE
£1.25
INCLUDING VAT

Tues. Nov.
at 7.30 p.m. **5**
Doors open 7.00 p.m.

DOOR B

B 26

TO BE RETAINED

CITY (OVAL) HALL
SHEFFIELD

ASTRA INTERNATIONAL presents
ARGENT
IN CONCERT
with guests CLANCY

STALLS
in quadrophonic
£1.20
INCLUDING VAT

Tues. Dec.
at 7.30 p.m. 10
Doors open 7.00 p.m.

DOOR F

N 18

CITY (OVAL) HALL
SHEFFIELD

Peter Bowyer
presents
SUPERTRAMP
in concert

STALLS
£1.00
INCLUDING VAT

Thur. Jan.
7.30 p.m. 23

DOOR G

T 29

TO BE RETAINED

CITY (OVAL) HALL
SHEFFIELD

Adrian Hopkins
presents
THIN LIZZY

Grand Circle
£2.00
INCLUDING VAT

A 84

DOOR F

WED

NOV

23rd

7.30 p.m.

WARNING
Official programmes/posters on sale
ONLY INSIDE THE HALL
TO BE RETAINED

CITY (OVAL) HALL
SHEFFIELD

Virgins Records Crisis Concert
HATFIELD AND THE NORTH
GONG
Plus On Film
Mike Oldfield's Tubular Bells

GRAND CIRCLE
44p
INCLUDING VAT

Fri. April
at 7.30 p.m. 26
Doors open 7.00 p.m.

DOOR B

A 35

TO BE RETAINED

Below:
Roxy Music at
Sheffield City Hall –
October 22, 1973

Elton John at
Sheffield City Hall
– December 14,
1973

★FROM BOUNCER TO SOCIAL SCIENCE UNDERGRADUATE

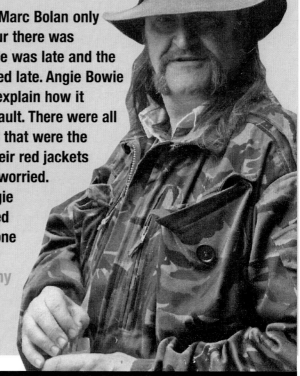

Having to be 'signed in' by a student to get access to student bars and gigs was the scourge of seventies Sheffield. But there were other ways.

Martin Bellamy: "After we'd visited the likes of Buccaneer, Nelson and Sportsman we'd go up to the university because every Saturday night there'd be a massive band on. You'd have to get a student to sign you in and half the a**eholes wouldn't do it.

"It so happened that this lass I knew had got a job in the university office and me and two of my mates said 'can you get us a union card?'. She handed us these three application forms and said 'just put down you're doing social sciences – they never check it'.

Gigs by everyone from The Who to Deep Purple followed for three of the university's most popular undergraduates (due to their willingness to sign-in every other non-student they could find).

★ "The night Marc Bolan only did half an hour there was nearly a riot. He was late and the gear had arrived late. Angie Bowie was trying to explain how it weren't their fault. There were all these old guys that were the stewards in their red jackets looking really worried. Thankfully Angie Bowie managed to calm everyone down."
Martin Bellamy

Right:
Martin Bellamy
as he is today

SPINNING THE DISCS
AT 'STEELY'S' AND 'IMPROVISION'

Many would argue that Sheffield's sprawling Top Rank was one of the UK's most successful discotheques of its time in the UK in the seventies.

The Arundel Gate venue – which years later became Roxy and was more recently re-born as the Academy – was regularly pulling in anything up to 2,500 punters every Saturday night at its renowned 'Steely's' night in the heady days of the 1970s.

The chain was also running dance halls in Birmingham, Southampton, Swansea, Cardiff, Plymouth and Reading, but Sheffield dwarfed the lot in terms of size.

Running from 8pm until 2am, 'Steely's' had a hardcore and loyal following from Sheffield and South Yorkshire but disco-goers would regularly travel from much further afield.

Even as far back as 1977 they were boasting £35,000 worth of sound and lighting equipment that created the pulsating carnage, turning the venue into a Pied Piper of seventies clubbing of garish and unrelenting proportions.

Left:
'Steely's' DJ
Reg Cliff
(left)

Right:
A very young Tony Beesley (left) and friend John Harrison on one of their first visits to Sheffield's pubs

Joanna English, then 19 years of age and residing in Mosborough, was one of its biggest fans.

She said at the time: "You can lose yourself here, it's so big. It's a fantastic atmosphere.

"At other places they say you can't do this and you can't do that. But if you're having a good time here, just enjoying yourself, other people will join in. Some nights you remember for ages afterwards."

For the majority it was their first proper foray into nightclub land, with the average age being between 18 and 21 years old.

Reg Cliff: "I deejayed as a part-time job at the Top Rank for two years, early 1977 to April 1979, and did most of the Saturday nights which were billed as 'Steely's', together with another DJ, Stewart McEgan.

★ **"Blacks and whites mix all right. If you want to see race equality working well in Sheffield, come to 'Steely's'."**
DJ Stuart McEgan

"I had previously deejayed at Baileys on Bank Street where we had a go-go dancer who performed in a cage.

"She loved Wild Cherry's 'Play That Funky Music'.

"I auditioned for the Rank and was told to play three records with introductions and a bit of chat.

"I remember playing Wings' 'Silly Love Songs' and Leo Sayer's 'You Make Me Feel Like Dancing'. I can't remember the other one. I thought I did quite well. I didn't make any gaffes, the patter was short but sweet and I cued the 45s up and segued them pretty well. I got the job.

"At that time disco music was massive. It had started to take

over the charts and the clubs from around '75 and during the time I was there we had 'Saturday Night Fever'."

You'd be lucky to find a nightclub that would even bother opening on a Christmas Eve in Sheffield 2010. It's a fact that many northern cities turn into ghost towns whilst nearby towns – Chesterfield for example – are madder than the wild west.

Things were rather different in the seventies.

Reg Cliff: "The Rank could hold up to 2,500 people on a Saturday night and was always sold out at Christmas and New Year's Eve. For sheer numbers, no other club in the area could compete.

"It wasn't just a disco though. We often put on special events such as dance competitions and also PA appearances by pop stars and groups who were in concert somewhere in the area - I remember The Dooleys being with us one Saturday night!

"We'd get them on stage for a quick interview, play their music a fair bit in the build-up before they came on and give away some of their records, or other goodies like badges and posters.

"We had big one-off promotional nights where the record companies would provide us with plenty of stuff to give away. I remember 'Saturday Night Fever' and 'Grease' as two of the biggest 'Steely's' nights we did.

Unlike the meteoric rise of the DJ during the clubbing explosion of the mid-1990s, Reg Cliff is the

first to admit that the DJ of the seventies was often thought of as one notch up from the cleaner in many cases.

Whilst a modern day DJ would rather burn in hell rather than bow to audience pressure to repeat a tune in any one set, it was common currency at 'Steely's'.

Reg Cliff: "Stewart and I would play the most popular records sometimes five or six times in a single evening. I well recall this being the case with songs such as Sylvester's 'You Make Me Feel (Mighty Real)', Boney M's 'Daddy Cool', Rose Royce's 'Car Wash' and Donna Summer's 'I Feel Love' and 'Love's Unkind'. The music was very much chart-based and poppy but we'd also play little sections of soul, Motown, funk and reggae."

The DJ was also responsible for doing more than keeping the dance floor moving in time – their elevated position and dulcet tones over the PA meant they were also the eyes and ears of the place.

Reg Cliff: "If you saw any trouble developing on the dance floor you had to alert the bouncers with a special code. I think there were five bars around the venue so if there was a fight in bar one you would say 'bar one, bar one, gentleman please". And if you were on the dance floor and you spotted it, it was bar six and the exit door was bar seven or something like that. Very sort of calm and reserved so no one would pick up and understand what you meant."

The venue was also doing its bit for racial harmony according to DJ Stuart McEgan at the time.

He said: "Blacks and whites mix all right. If you want to see racial equality working well in Sheffield, come to 'Steely's'."

★A DOOMED LEPPARD AT DIAL HOUSE

Reg Cliff: "Sometime in late '77 I was with friends at Dial House Social Club to watch Bitter Suite play. Before they came on stage a couple of youngsters, recognising me as the DJ from 'Improvision', came over and started to tell me about the heavy rock band they'd recently formed. They told me who their influences were and that they'd written their own material and wanted to get some gigs locally. They asked if I could get them a support slot at Improvision. I told them that I didn't

have any say in that department but I'd have a word with the Rank's general manager which is what I did. Nothing came of it. However, they did play the Rank at a later time as well as some of the biggest arenas in the world. The kid who did most of the talking was Joe Elliott. I squirm with embarrassment when I recall asking him what the band was called. Def Leppard, he replied. 'What a daft name', I thought, 'they'll never make it with a name like that'. Whoops!"

★'IMPROVISION'

Top Rank, being the money making machine it was, was never going to be satisfied with just cashing in on mainstream audiences.

As well as an 'over 25s' night event, it actually nurtured one of the best alternative/rock nights of the era in the shape of 'Improvision' – another night Reg Cliff worked at.

Reg Cliff: 'Improvision' was the name given to gig-based Sunday nights at the Rank from about 1977 onwards. There had been Sunday night gigs before that, but I think that the management invented the name 'Improvision' to give Sunday night a stronger identity. I deejayed most of the Sundays and the bands were principally new wave or punk with some heavy rock too. AC/DC, Judas Priest and Styx all played there. So did The Adverts, The Vibrators, Penetration and Buzzcocks as well as Dave Edmunds, Nick Lowe and the Steve Gibbons Band. When The Jam and The Stranglers appeared it was packed out. If you were stood upstairs you could feel the floor moving due to the number of people who jumped and pogoed along to the music!

"My diary tells me that Magazine played 'Improvision' on 23/7/78 with The Motors as support. Magazine were promoting their 'Real Life' album, widely admired by the music critics. They'd had a minor hit single earlier the same year with 'Shot By Both Sides'. Howard Devoto, formerly of the Buzzcocks, was the main man. The Motors played their support slot including their big hit single 'Airport' which wasn't really representative of their sound. I went into Magazine's dressing room to tell them that they would be on in five minutes and accidentally interrupted Howard Devoto who was in full flow, slagging off 'Airport'. He hated it, big time."

Supercharge perform at 'Improvision'

Above: The Maurice Naylor Band at Top Rank

★ "I went into Magazine's dressing room to tell them that they would be on in five minutes and accidentally interrupted Howard Devoto who was in full flow, slagging off 'Airport'. He hated it, big time."

Reg Cliff

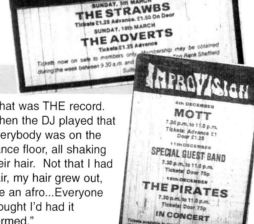

IMPROVISION

SUNDAY, 5th MARCH
THE STRAWBS
Tickets £1.25 Advance. £1.50 On Door
SUNDAY, 19th MARCH
THE ADVERTS
Tickets £1.25 Advance

Tickets now on sale to members only. Membership may be obtained during the week between 9.30 a.m. and [...] Top Rank Sheffield

IMPROVISION

4th DECEMBER
MOTT
7.30 p.m. to 11.0 p.m.
Tickets: Advance £1
Door £1.25
11th DECEMBER
SPECIAL GUEST BAND
7.30 p.m. to 11.0 p.m.
Tickets: Door 75p
18th DECEMBER
THE PIRATES
7.30 p.m. to 11.0 p.m.
Tickets: Door 75p
IN CONCERT

Tickets available to members only. Membership may be obtained starting the week [...]

★MORE TALES OF AFTER DARK ACTION

When Reg wasn't spinning the discs at Top Rank or going clothes shopping at Burtons or Harringtons in Castle Market he was keeping up to speed with happenings around the rest of town.

Reg Cliff: "Crazy Daizy was always a good place. It had a low ceiling like The Limit. It had that sort of intimate sweaty club atmosphere and because Ray Stewart was a DJ there it was even better because I loved him - I thought he was great.

"It was just in stark contrast to The Rank."

By the late seventies and the rise of punk there was a sharp contrast in types of punter and type of venues – you were either going to mainstream and adhering to strict dress policies of places like Josephines and Scamps or you were going to places like The Limit or Wapentake with zero dress policy (though you'd probably be

refused entry if you turned up in a suit and tie).

Reg was one of the few that used to try everything.

"I wouldn't mind going to Josephine's or Genevieve and the other one behind Genevieve, Mona Lisa."

Reg, like many, was also a regular at Tivoli in Fitzalan Square.

"I used to go in there because I'm a united fan and we used to go in there before the match on a Saturday lunchtime. Chip butty and a few games of pool."

He also frequented The Penthouse – nightclub's answer to running a half-marathon before you even entered thanks to the endless amounts of steps you had to climb to get up there.

"The Penthouse was a bit like The Wapentake but darker and probably messier as well. Beer slops all over the floor. One record that always reminds me of it is Rainbow's 'Stargazer'.

"That was THE record. When the DJ played that everybody was on the dance floor, all shaking their hair. Not that I had hair, my hair grew out, like an afro...Everyone thought I'd had it permed."

★Chris Wintle

"I was a regular at the rock night at Top Rank called 'Improvision'. It was just before the punk explosion. I remember seeing The Police there before they got big – they were absolutely brilliant. I saw The Stranglers as well. There'd probably be 400 to 500 in – mostly Wapentake-types. It showcased a massive list of bands that were about to make it, or those that were already making it.

"I remember it lasted a good couple of years. We'd normally go to The Mulberry across the road for a drink beforehand. They were one of the few places selling Newcastle Exhibition beer."

Right: Top Rank – now Academy via its infamous years as The Roxy

★STARTING LIFE AT TOP RANK

Phil Staniland: "The first town disco I went in was at the Top Rank in my early teens. They used to have a Tuesday night - non alcohol night that was for school kids really that we all went to at the time. When I say 'we' I mean kids in my school year and in Pitsmoor where I lived. At the time this was a really impressive experience for us as it seemed really hi tech and 'grown up'. There were lots of nice girls there who all smoked Players No 6 which made them seem as if they were in their 20s or 30s when in actual fact they were probably the same age as us.

"While I was at school in year four or five I used to go to the 'Improvision' which was just fantastic at the time. This was every Sunday night at the Top Rank and

was just as punk was developing. They always had a live band on and a great disco. For a Sunday night it was always jam packed and a great atmosphere.

"I saw a lot of the punk bands here in their early stages i.e. The Stranglers, The Jam, Buzzcocks, The Drones, The Clash, Ramones, The Vibrators, Sham 69, Richard Hell and the Voidoids etc, etc; plus they had other sort of off the wall bands on like Split Enz and Deaf School. It really was quite an eclectic evening because it was caught in the middle of the inevitable punk explosion and the sounds of before, or pre-punk if you like. It really was an incredible scene when you were still at school and I wasn't even old enough to get in. I used to use my friend's older brother's membership card to gain entry.

★ **"There were lots of nice girls there who all smoked Players No. 6 which made them seem as if they were in their 20s or 30s when in actual fact they were probably the same age as us."**

Phil Staniland

"As a result of my great 'Improvision' memories I have always had a soft spot for this venue even when it was Roxys and drawing in Flower Estate clientele. Consequently it was a great privilege to play the venue during the Rock n Pop Contest of 1982 and on other nights after the competition. I wish they could start that night off again, although I'm not sure it would fit in now. Anyone who ever went to the 'Improvision' who you meet now always have fond memories of it. It was the place I first saw people pogoing and wondered at the time what the hell they were doing as it was so new!!!

"After that my pub/club years didn't start until about circa late '78 in my first year at college. "Religiously we always went to the Wapentake, The Nelson, and The Penthouse (which was what became Rebels)."

★Nigel Lockwood

"Bowie was the instigator of a lot of music and fashion trends that influenced everything else in the era.

"Seeing David Bowie at the Top Rank on September 6, 1972, was the thing that changed everything for me – that and seeing him perform 'Star Man' on Top Of The Pops.

"What that did for a lot of other people is made them form bands.

"The only merchandise on sale were two posters – I've still got them both. That was the first rock gig I went to. The second was The Faces at Sheffield City Hall in December 1972. They came on at 10pm and Rod Stewart was kicking footballs out into the audience.

"The other major gig that really affected me was Mick Ronson at Sheffield City Hall in April 1974 and after that we all went back to the Hallam Towers Hotel to see him.

"Then Roxy Music had more of an influence. I also saw Lou Reed at Sheffield City Hall, Brian Eno do one of his rare shows and Status Quo who were brilliant at the time. Sparks, Elton John, Mott The Hoople and Cockney Rebel, who I loved.

"Then came pub rock bands like Doctor Feelgood and the Kursaal Flyers in 1975 that I saw at the Black Swan – they kind of set the genre for what influenced the punk bands in the year after."

The author

Neil Anderson first launched Sheffield's Dirty Stop Out's Guide(TM) in 1994. His dedication to the cause has seen him leave no bar stool unturned in his insatiable thirst for knowledge.

Though he was only just out of nappies in 1970, his 'Take It To The Limit' book about legendary West Street club The Limit became a best seller in 2009 closely followed by his 'Shopaholics Guide to 1970s Sheffield' which was released the same year.

Neil has written on nightlife and entertainment for titles spanning The Independent to The Big Issue and was a Sheffield Telegraph columnist for 12 years.

When he's not writing books about nightlife venues he's busy promoting them and other businesses through his All Credit Media communications agency (www.allcreditmedia.com).

Acknowledgements

Sheffield Newspapers for use of their wonderful pics and articles, Sheffield Local Studies Library for help digging out articles and pics, Sheffield City Council, Martin Bellamy and Sara Parkes for words and weather reports, Olga Marshall, Paul Unwin, Pete Gill, Dave Berry, Clive Porter, Andy Smith, Chris Wintle, Phil Staniland, Peter McNerney, Ian Gomm, Peter Wigley, Diana Collins, Bitter Suite, Marie-Luise Coulthard, Martin Smith, Martin Dawes, Dave Allen, Julie Batty, Jane Salt, Graham Walker, Doug and Denise Huntingdon, Rachael Hope, Keith Skues, Pete Hill, Dave Kilner RIP, Julie Wilson, Tony Beesley, Reg Cliff, Terry and Nicola Steeples, Brendan Moffett, Steve Stevlor, Orrett and Jacqueline Hanson, Glen Matlock, Christine Ward, Simon Milner, Nigel Lockwood and a memorabilia collection that rivals Ohio's Rock and Roll Hall of Fame, Caroline Gowing, Barry Everard, Tony Beesley, the girls at The Star Shop, Sheryl Littlewood, Jackie Stanley, John Turnball, Judi Emm, Bailey Brothers, Dave Muscroft (www.davidmuscroft.com), Mel Day, John and Lynda Mitchell, Jon Downing, Debra Marshall, Stuart Smith and Haydn Anderson who's still finding fault with his son's grammar god knows how many years on.

Inspiration, proofing and transcriptions beyond the call of duty: **Lindsay McLaren.**
All round inspiration: **Lowri and Ewan Anderson.**

Photography, proofing and balancing the books: **Ian Cheetham.**
Book design and layout: **Afb Creatives.**
Mail order: **Karen Davies.**

The Dirty Stop Out's Guide trademark is owned by Neil Anderson and licensed to ACM Retro Ltd.

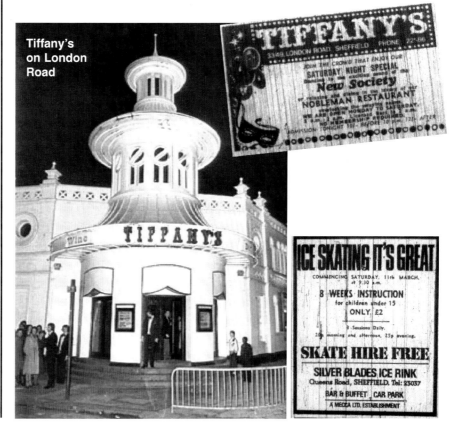

Tiffany's on London Road

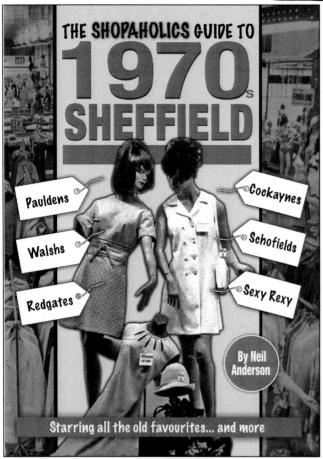
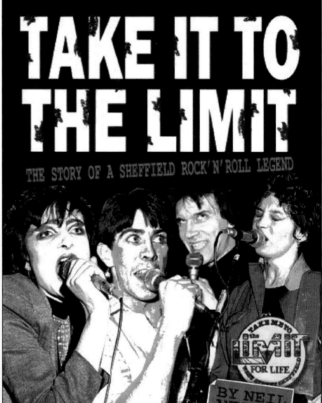

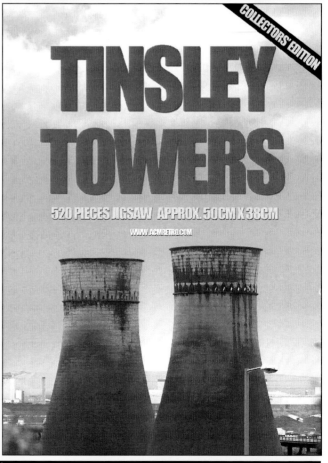